# BUILDING
# BRIDGES

*Fouad Elias Accad*

# BUILDING

# BRIDGES

## CHRISTIANITY AND ISLAM

NAVPRESS

A MINISTRY OF THE NAVIGATORS
P.O. BOX 35001, COLORADO SPRINGS, COLORADO 80935

## OUR GUARANTEE TO YOU

We believe so strongly in the message of our books that we are making this quality guarantee to you. If for any reason you are disappointed with the content of this book, return the title page to us with your name and address and we will refund to you the list price of the book. To help us serve you better, please briefly describe why you were disappointed. Mail your refund request to: NavPress, P.O. Box 35002, Colorado Springs, CO 80935.

© 1997 by Bridges of Peace International
All rights reserved. No part of this publication may be reproduced in any form without written
       permission from NavPress, P.O. Box 35001, Colorado Springs, CO 80935.
Library of Congress Catalog Card Number: 96-36968
ISBN 08910-97953

Cover photo by Planet Art

Some of the anecdotal illustrations in this book are true to life and are included with the permission of the persons involved. All other illustrations are composites of real situations, and any resemblance to people living or dead is coincidental.

Unless otherwise identified, all Scripture quotations in this publication are taken from the *HOLY BIBLE: NEW INTERNATIONAL VERSION*® (NIV®). Copyright © 1973, 1978, 1984, International Bible Society. Used by permission of Zondervan Bible Publishing House. All rights reserved. Other version used: *King James Version.*

Unless otherwise identified, quotations from the Koran are from *The Koran Interpreted*, translated by A.J. Arberry, Copyright © 1955 by George Allen and Unwin Ltd., reprinted with the permission of Simon & Schuster, New York, and with the permission of HarperCollins Publishers Ltd., London. Other version used: *The Koran*, translated by N.J. Dawood, copyright © N.J. Dawood 1956, 1959, 1966, 1968, 1974, 1990, 1993, published by the Penguin Group, London.

Accad, Fouad Elias.
       Building bridges : Christianity and Islam / Found Elias Accad.
       p.    cm.
       ISBN 0-89109-795-3
1. Islam—Relations—Christianity.  2. Christianity and other religions—Islam. I. Title.
BP172.A.27    1997
266',0088'2971—dc21

                                                                                                    96-36968
                                                                                                    CIP

Printed in the United States of America

2 3 4 5 6 7 8 9 10 11/04 03 02 01 00 99

FOR A FREE CATALOG OF
NAVPRESS BOOKS & BIBLE STUDIES,
CALL 1-800-366-7788 (USA)
or 1-416-499-4615 (CANADA)

# Contents

❦

# CHAPTER 1

# New Fruitfulness Among Muslims

∽✝∾

Mr. A heard the gospel preached in a large meeting in a Middle Eastern country. Deeply moved, he entrusted his life to Christ and experienced an immediate peace and joy. He ran to tell his family, adding that he had never been this close to God, and that he had now found the true way to God. They threatened to kill him for such blasphemy and locked him out of the house, telling him he was no longer part of their family and that he was never to return. The Christians in the nearby church helped him, and praised him for "suffering for Christ."

He went on to preach Christ publicly to nominal Christians and Muslims there until he had to leave the country to protect his life. Upon arrival in the United States, he immediately became a celebrity in the Christian community, was given many speaking engagements, and was exalted in a prominent evangelical seminary for his faithful stand under persecution for Christ.

But his chances to communicate with Muslims ever again were nil. His family and friends back home considered him an apostate and would have nothing to do with him. If he dared return, he would probably do so at the loss of his life. In some countries, the penalty for officially converting to Christianity can be death.

Conversion is seen by them as becoming a traitor to family, clan, tribe, people, country, and race.

Ninety-five percent of the few Muslims who do come to Christ tell stories of ill-treatment by their families and former friends within days of revealing their decision to "become a Christian."

The irony in all this is that following Christ should not — and *need* not — bring on persecution and blame from other Muslims, since Christ is considered one of the greatest prophets in the Qur'an (sometimes spelled "Koran"), the foremost holy book of Islam. Since this is indeed the case, what is the need for a Muslim to unnecessarily intimidate and alienate his fellow Muslims when he becomes a follower of Christ? If a Muslim could trust Christ without alienating his family and friends, he could become a means within his own community to testify to them about the extraordinary blessings they can obtain from knowing Christ better as the One who is so highly exalted by their own Qur'an. As it is, because of what he suffers physically and emotionally, the convert may succeed in impressing Western Christians, but he is totally cut off from having any influence on his own people.

Today there are Muslims trusting Christ in Muslim lands who do not consider that they have become "Christians" (the word has a political connotation to Muslims), but instead see themselves as having become truly Muslim (the word *Muslim* means "surrendered to God"). These new believers in Christ are reading the Bible with their Muslim friends, and no one has kicked them out of their homes and communities, for they are not viewed as traitors. How has this happened?

Muslims believe there is one way — *God's* way. So if someone comes saying, "Islam is all wrong. 'Allah' is not God. You have to accept Jesus, God's Son. He's the only way to God," a Muslim turns him off at once because he is contradicting what the Muslim has been taught as God's holy truth. But suppose you say, "I agree. There is only one way — God's way." You are careful not to quote John 3:16 unnecessarily because once a Muslim hears the words

"God's Son," he is horrified. (He assumes that you mean that God had intercourse with a woman who might happen to have been Mary, Jesus' mother.)

Instead, you quote John 1:1-2: "In the beginning was the Word, and the Word was with God, and the Word was God. He was with God in the beginning." The Qur'an also says that Jesus is the Word of God, so this is an acceptable idea and wording. (See Women 4:171: "The Messiah, Jesus son of Mary, was . . . the Messenger of God, and His Word that He committed to Mary, and a Spirit from Him.")

"Now, which came first, God or His Word?" you ask the seeking Muslim. "Well, of course, God came first; nothing came before Him," he answers. You ask, "But was He mute? Could He not speak? Was He imperfect?" He replies, "Of course, God has never had any imperfections. He could speak at all times."

So it is easy to explain to him that God's Word is included in His essence, that no one can separate God from His Word. And so Christ's deity is for the first time a possibility because it fits with the teaching of the Muslim's holy book.

For centuries, missionaries, following in the steps of their great reformers, have viewed the Qur'an as a devilish book, without ever studying it for themselves. They don't realize that Muhammad brought the Qur'an, in Arabic, to the Arabs because the Jews had their book (the Old Testament) in their language and the Christians had their book (the Bible) in their languages and yet the Arabs did not have any "Book" in their language. (See Poets 26:192-199: "Truly it [the Qur'an] is the revelation of the Lord of all Being, brought down by the Faithful Spirit upon thy heart [Muhammad], that thou mayest be one of the warners, in a clear, Arabic tongue. Truly it [the Qur'an] is in the Scriptures [the Bible] of the ancients [it is not something new]. Was it not a sign [proof] for them, that it is known to the learned [knowledgeable] of the Children of Israel? If We [God] had sent it down on a barbarian [a non-Arab] and he had recited it to them, they would not have believed in it [for lack of understanding its language].") A lot of what Muhammad quoted in the Qur'an comes from what he heard from the Jews and Christians he met in Arabia.

As I've studied the Qur'an for thirty years, I've found it overwhelmingly pro-Christ, pro-Christian, and pro-Bible. So just as your witness is enhanced when you quote a highly respected secular leader who makes a pro-Christian statement, so the Qur'an can greatly influence Muslims to consider Christ. For example, the Qur'an says, "When the angels said, 'Mary, God gives thee good tidings of a Word from Him whose name is Messiah, Jesus, son of Mary; high honoured shall he be in this world and the next, near stationed to God'" (House of Imran 3:45). By pointing this out to the Muslim who sincerely wants to please God (and many do), he becomes very interested in learning more about Jesus, for a Muslim wants someone to intercede for him. And who would be in a better position to do so than Jesus, who is near-stationed to God?

In one Middle Eastern country, thirty to thirty-five Muslims have believed in Christ as their redeemer and intercessor while remaining in the fold of their Islamic community for a span of eight years. In fact, we have found that 60 percent of Muslims who are approached with the method explained in this book put their trust in Christ—and all who do, do so without becoming detestable to their own communities.

The purpose of this book is to build bridges between two communities—Muslim and Christian. Bridges of understanding, communication, and certainly love. It provides personal experiences based on a lifetime of ministry to the Arab world, as well as research and analysis of the texts of the Qur'an and the Bible to show the similarities between the two. When we reach out to Muslims to build such a bridge, we need to provide information, concrete examples, and insights in order to help those who are seeking truth.

Missionaries to Muslim lands seldom see more than a handful of people come to Christ after decades of hard labor. This book seeks to explore some of the reasons for such misunderstandings and offer practical help to anyone who wants to be a bridge-builder to the precious Muslim people. The misunderstandings that have built walls instead of bridges between Western culture and Arab-Muslim culture must, from God's perspective, be one of the tragedies of our times.

If we're going to build bridges to Christ for the worldwide Muslim population (which constitutes a fifth of the world population), we desperately need to use a method that taps into their very real desire to please God. It is incredibly good news to a conscientious Muslim who has put his trust in Christ as Redeemer that he can know that his sins are forgiven, that he will assuredly go to heaven, and that he can have nothing to fear on Judgment Day—and still be a part of his community! But unfortunately our methods of communicating these truths in the past have so offended the vast majority of Muslims that they totally close their minds and become hostile to us. Our insensitive approach is one of the things that has kept seeking people from the liberating truth. How tragic! The harvest is ripe. There is an exciting new fruitfulness among Muslims. Who shall gather in the harvest?

Here in this book you will find a radically different, scriptural means of telling Muslims who Christ actually is and why He occupies such a prominent place in their Qur'an—without alienating them from their native culture. We should be encouraging them to continue living among their own people as witnesses to Christ's power of reconciliation, reaching out to their neighbors and friends. Only when they become salt and light in this way will *we* be truly salt and light for the living God.

# CHAPTER 2
# The Qur'an as a Bridge to the Bible

࿔

The Bible contains many passages that teach us how to approach people of different cultures and customs with the good news of salvation. We are specifically instructed to present our message "with gentleness and respect" (1 Peter 3:15). When we approach Muslims, we are dealing with a culture where honor and respect are of utmost importance.

Accordingly, it would be insensitive — in fact, negligent — if we were to completely disregard the Qur'an. Why? Because it would be difficult, if not impossible, to discuss spiritual things with Muslims if we ignore their primary spiritual guidebook. It would be a case of conspicuous omission. A Muslim would have great difficulty embracing the message behind your words from the Bible — even though it is a book highly revered in Islamic religion and culture — until you show him or her how those words relate to the Qur'an.

How can we connect with someone from another culture unless we first establish common ground with that person's culture and traditions? We see an example of such a cultural bridge when the apostle Paul arrived in Athens to present the good news of salvation to the philosophers and the idol-worshiping people of that culturally rich city (Acts 17).

## Cultural Adaptation

First, notice that when Paul was in Thessalonica on his way to Athens, he met with fellow Jews on their own turf, the synagogue (Acts 17:1-2). Second, he didn't say, "Come worship with us on Sunday" (the Christian day of worship), but instead went to their place of worship on *their* holy day. By working among them from the inside of their religious and national life, he made such an impact that many of them came to believe the good news—not only Jews, but a great many of the foreigners who were living there (17:4).

The application for us? How can we expect to win Muslims from the *outside*? Too often we come across as the all-knowing Westerners, insisting on displacing the cultural and religious customs of people in the Middle East with our own cultural and religious traditions. We unwittingly say to them, "You are Muslims. We are Western Christians. You have to come to us and follow our ways. If you do not adapt to our culture and customs, you cannot become members of God's people."

We don't come right out and say it in those actual words, but our methods and lifestyles imply it. A common example is a new believer from a Muslim family being outraged by the proud and "unclean" way Christians worship when men and women sit next to each other (which, according to the Muslim mind-set, leads to immorality) and people fail to wash their feet, their arms, and other exposed parts of their bodies before entering the place of worship (making them ritually unclean from a Muslim point of view). And they dare to sit upright with crossed legs while talking to Almighty God, thus showing their pride, whereas a Muslim prostrates himself when he prays to show his deep-felt humility before God.

In contrast, assemblies of Muslims who become believers in Isa (the Qur'anic word for Jesus) tend to adapt their worship to Muslim culture and customs. For example, they meet on Friday, the Muslim holy day, and a facility for washing prior to prayer is provided outside the entrance. Believers remove their shoes and sit on the floor during the sermon as they were accustomed to do in the mosque. They use Muslim prayer posture and dress in typical Muslim clothing. A wooden stand is used as a Bible-holder, similar to the one used for the Qur'an in the mosque. All this adaptation in forms of worship tends to make Muslims comfortable enough to attend services, and eventually many of them come to the point where they pray in Christ's name and are born anew.

To many of us, all these ceremonial observances might seem unnecessary and even restrictive. We may think of passages from the Bible that seem to contradict such practices: "If the Son sets you free, you will be free indeed" (John 8:36), or, "Do not let anyone judge you by what you eat or drink, or with regard to a religious festival, a New Moon celebration or a Sabbath day. These are a shadow of the things that were to come; the reality, however, is found in Christ" (Colossians 2:16-17).

But there are other Bible passages that are more directly relevant to the context I am describing, where the behavior and setting take on different meaning and proportions:

Accept him whose faith is weak, without passing judgment on disputable matters. One man's faith allows him to eat everything, but another man, whose faith is weak, eats only vegetables. (Romans 14:1-2)

If your brother is distressed because of what you eat, you are no longer acting in love. Do not by your eating destroy your brother for whom Christ died. (Romans 14:15)

I try to please everybody in every way. For I am not seeking my own good but the good of many, so that they may be saved. (1 Corinthians 10:33)

We put no stumbling block in anyone's path, so that our ministry will not be discredited. Rather, as servants of God we commend ourselves in every way: in great endurance; in troubles, hardships and distresses. (2 Corinthians 6:3-4)

What Paul seems to be saying is not to make an issue of personal preferences and opinions when it comes to the outward environment or "forms" of worship. At the same time, we should be careful not to impose our own Western cultural tastes or style of leadership on the group that is gathered for worship in a Middle Eastern country. Instead, we should let them make their own choices about what is best for their situation and what follows the spirit of their own culture and customs. Otherwise, they may feel such extreme cultural discomfort that any future opportunities to reach them with the gospel would be lost.

We should always keep in mind that in each country of the Muslim world there are many groups and sects, each with different ways of thinking, worshiping, and doing things. Certain things one group follows because it suits them may not be suitable for another group. This is also true on a much larger scale from one country to another throughout the Muslim world.

An example of inappropriate cultural application is that of a missionary in Aden, Yemen, who started a carefully contextualized worship environment to make Muslims feel comfortable in the way that I just mentioned. This was many years before any missionary efforts were made in that city. I was astonished to hear a Muslim teacher complain one day to some of his friends about this missionary's non-Western methods, saying with irony in his voice, "Now that we have started to sit comfortably on chairs and eat properly behind attractive tables, this missionary wants to send us back to the ancient times of ignorance and savagery!" And so we see that each cultural context must be examined thoroughly before we rush in with our preconceived ideas.

## Starting Where People Are: Paul in the Synagogue

While in the synagogue in Thessalonica, Paul didn't talk initially to the Jews about Jesus of Nazareth, who was a stranger to them, but he started with Christ (the Messiah) and what their scripture (the Old Testament) said about His predicted sufferings, death, and resurrection. After that, he introduced Jesus of Nazareth as being the fulfillment of these prophecies. As a result, some Jews and many God-fearing non-Jews accepted Jesus as the Messiah (Acts 17:4).

Using Paul's method, we can introduce accurate verses about Christ from the Qur'an to Muslims, which will naturally arouse their respect for what Muhammad has brought them and at the same time open a door of curiosity about the full identity of Jesus Christ. But we must first reinforce their comfort zone with truth from the Qur'an before we try to expose them to the fuller truth from the Bible. When some of the Muslims object, saying, "But what authority do you have from the Muslim leaders permitting you to make such interpretation of our Book?" I answer: "Was it valid for the early Christians to apply Old Testament Messianic prophecies to Jesus of Nazareth, as we see in the New Testament, without first receiving permission from Jewish leaders?" Understanding and personal application of such material is a common heritage of all humanity.

But let's back up for a moment. We need to take a look at the historical context of the whole Bible. It is obvious that the relation between the Old Testament (the Tawrah, or the Torah) and the New Testament (the Injeel) is an organic one because both came from the same Source (God) and were used, especially at the beginning, by the same peoples. Consequently, when the Christian church became firmly established, the Christian believers decided to add the books of the New Testament to those of the Old Testament, declaring the whole corpus under the name of "Bible" to be the one and only canon of divinely inspired Scriptures (see Revelation 22:18-19).

However, the relation between the Bible and the Qur'an is quite a bit different. The biblical passages found now in the Qur'an are only a rendering in Arabic of what the Jews and Christians taught Muhammad. Many passages in the Qu'ran speak about this matter and how it was finally dealt with. It can be clearly seen in the following passages of Sura 2 (the Cow) and Sura 5 (the Table)

("Sura" means Qur'anic chapter). Please note that the explanations within brackets are mine, added for clarity:

> Children of Israel, remember the favour I have bestowed upon you. Keep your covenant, and I will be true to Mine. Dread My power [have awe of God]. Have faith in My revelations [or, in Arberry, "what I have sent down"—the Qur'an], which confirm your Scriptures [the Tawrat], and do not be the first to deny them. (Cow 2:40-41, Dawood)

> And now that a Book [the Qur'an] confirming their own has come to them ["Children of Israel"] from God, they deny it, although they know it to be the truth and have long prayed for help against the unbelievers. (Cow 2:89, Dawood)

> When they [the Jews] are told: "Believe in what God has revealed" [the Qur'an], they reply: "We believe in what was revealed to *us*." But they deny what has since been revealed, although it is the truth, corroborating their own scriptures. (Cow 2:91, Dawood)

> When there has come to them [the Jews and the Christians] a Messenger from God [Muhammad] confirming what was with them, a party of them [the Jews] that were given the Book [the Qur'an] reject [throw away] the Book of God [the Qur'an] behind their backs, as though they knew not. (Cow 2:101)

> Yet how will they [the Jews] make thee [Muhammad] their judge seeing they have the Torah, wherein is God's judgment . . . ? Surely We [God] sent down the Torah, wherein is guidance and light; thereby the Prophets who had surrendered themselves gave judgment for those of Jewry, as did the masters and the rabbis, following such

portion of God's Book as they were given to keep and were witnesses to. So fear not men, but fear you Me; and sell not My signs for a little price. Whoso judges not according to what God has sent down—they are the unbelievers. (Table 5:43-44)

So let the People of the Gospel [of the Injeel—the Christians] judge according to what God has sent down therein. Whosoever judges not according to what God has sent down—they are the ungodly. (Table 5:47)

Believers [the Muslims], Jews, Sabaeans [probably the Subba, disciples of John the Baptist—Yahya] and Christians—whoever believes in God and the Last Day and does what is right—shall have nothing to fear or to regret. (Table 5:69, Dawood)

The nearest in affection to them [Muslims] are those who say: "We are Christians." That is because there are priests and monks among them; and because they are free from pride. (Table 5:82, Dawood)

## The Friendly Approach:
## Paul Speaks to the People of Athens

Paul rose to speak to the crowd gathered in the legendary Athenian courtyard where once stood the great Greek philosophers. In the following passage from the book of Acts, Luke re-creates the dramatic scene where Paul shows his facility for captivating a crowd of intellectuals:

Paul then stood up in the meeting of the Areopagus and said: "Men of Athens! I see that in every way you are very religious. For as I walked around and looked carefully at your objects of worship, I even found an altar with this inscription: TO AN UNKNOWN GOD. Now what you worship as something unknown I am going to proclaim to you.

"The God who made the world and everything in it is the Lord of heaven and earth and does not live in temples built by hands. And he is not served by human hands, as if he needed anything, because he himself gives all men life and breath and everything else. From one man he made every nation of men, that they should inhabit the whole earth; and he determined the times set for them and the exact places where they should live. God did this so that men would seek him and perhaps reach out for him and find him, though he is not far from each one of us. 'For in him we live and move and have our being.' As some of your own poets have said, 'We are his offspring.'

"Therefore since we are God's offspring, we should not think that the divine being is like gold or silver or stone—an image made by man's design and skill. In the past God overlooked such ignorance, but now he commands all people everywhere to repent. For he has set a day when he will judge the world with justice by the man he has appointed. He has given proof of this to all men by raising him from the dead."

When they heard about the resurrection of the dead, some of them sneered, but others said, "We want to hear you again on this subject." At that, Paul left the Council. A few men became followers of Paul and believed. Among them was Dionysius, a member of the Areopagus, also a woman named Damaris, and a number of others. (Acts 17:22-34)

This account of Paul's journey to Athens can teach us many valuable lessons for Christian-Muslim relations. The Greek religion Paul refers to in his address before the official council of Athens had very little in common with Christianity. God moved some of the people who were present at that speech to embrace the gospel message. Those people became some of the first corner-stones in one of the strongest world churches: the Greek Ortho-dox Church. It only stands to reason that the Lord can bring an even greater harvest of believers in today's world through the work of enthusiastic mission agencies and churches.

## The Responsible Approach:
## Paul Establishes Cultural Common Ground

> While Paul was waiting for them in Athens, he was greatly distressed to see that the city was full of idols. So he reasoned in the synagogue with the Jews and the God-fearing Greeks, as well as in the marketplace day by day with those who happened to be there. (Acts 17:16-17)

There Paul was, waiting in Athens for Silas and Timothy to arrive. He decided to walk around the city, but the more he saw, the more burdened he became. He saw idols—statues of empty gods and goddesses—everywhere he went, and people who were spiritually empty inside. Paul really cared about those people. His perspective was, "Who is weak, and I do not feel weak? Who is led into sin, and I do not inwardly burn?" (2 Corinthians 11:29). He must have prayed tenaciously for God to show him how to reach those people.

Seeing their raw heathen ways, Paul could have just as eas-ily addressed the Athenian people in the marketplace in this man-ner: "Oh, you foolish people of Athens! You have had so many philosophers and learned people who have left you great words of wisdom—Socrates, Plato, Aristotle. Why didn't you listen to them? You're just like the fools the Bible describes, people who make an idol out of wood or stone and then worship it, saying this is their god. And with the remaining wood left over from your carv-ing of the idol, you cook your dinner" (an adapted paraphrase of Isaiah 44:13-17).

But Paul didn't debase them or expose their foolishness in

such a derogatory way. When we put a sinner down, condemning him for his bad practices and erroneous beliefs, it's no wonder that person becomes angry and turns away, giving us no further chance to influence him. In contrast, we see Paul approaching the Athenians in a sympathetic and friendly manner, stating his case to them with illustrations from their own culture, examples surrounding them right there in the marketplace. He didn't begin right away with something foreign that they couldn't understand.

Notice his understanding of these idol-worshipers: "Men of Athens! I see that in every way you are very religious" (Acts 17:22). How could he genuinely feel such sympathy? The people were obviously worshiping idols and performing futile religious practices. Was Paul serious in approaching them with what seemed to be a commendation, or was he just trying to flatter them? Paul was not a deceiver. He was serious. Paul could see in their searching and their actions that their hearts were not satisfied. They were looking for the God who would satisfy their hearts' desires.

Some of us conclude that other people have worthless religious practices. The fact is, we have failed to realize that those people only do these things in an effort to please God, whom they appreciate and revere above everything else. Think of sincere, devout Muslims. They give to the poor. They fast from dawn to sundown for a whole month every year. They stop whatever they are doing five times a day to pray. They undergo ice-cold ablutions (if they are in cold countries), or rub themselves with scorching hot sand (if they are in desert lands) when they are not able to find water in preparation for these prayers. How many Christians, who are commanded to pray without ceasing (1 Thessalonians 5:17), pray that often?

Paul, instead of condemning the Athenians for their ineffective attempts to reach God, commended them for being "in every way . . . very religious," thus warming their hearts to his message. People tend to respond to someone who is genuinely sympathetic to them.

Paul followed this by saying, in essence, "You must be thinking about this unknown god a lot to have gone to all the trouble of building him an altar. Well, I have some very good news for you. I've come to tell you that this god that you seek is truly God."

It's interesting to observe that, in rejecting the Athenians' erroneous concept of God, Paul did not reject the word they used for God, *Theos*, which was the common Greek word for God. Some Christians unthinkingly say, "'Allah' is not God." This is the ultimate blasphemy to Muslims, and furthermore, it is difficult to understand. *Allah* is the primary Arabic word for God. It means "The God." There are some minor exceptions. For example, the Bible in some Muslim lands uses a word for God other than *Allah* (*Farsi* and *Urdu* are examples). But for more than five hundred years before Muhammad, the vast majority of Jews and Christians in Arabia called God by the name Allah. How, then, can we say that Allah is an invalid name for God? If it is, to whom have these Jews and Christians been praying?

And what about the 10 to 12 million Arab Christians today? They have been calling God "Allah" in their Bibles, hymns, poems, writings, and worship for over nineteen centuries. What an insult to them when we tell them not to use this word *Allah*! Instead of bridging the distance between Muslims and Christians, we widen the gulf of separation between them and us when we promote such a doctrine. Those who still insist that it is blasphemy to refer to God as Allah should also consider that Muhammad's father was named Abd Allah, "God's servant," many years before his son was born or Islam was founded!

Paul described God to his Athenian listeners in general terms that they were familiar with, using a reference to their philosophers and poets as a bridge to introduce them to a few quotations from the Old Testament about God. Then he followed with his declaration that Jesus Christ was the Savior of everyone in the world. It is worth noting that Paul did not hesitate to mention Greek poets in his declaration, though he was perfectly aware that these poets had been inspired by sister goddesses named Muse. It is worth noting that the Spirit of God, who inspired the writer of the book of Acts, did not hesitate to include a statement from one of these Greek poets in the content of the Bible.

It is in this light that the Christian can skillfully share truth from the Qur'an with his Muslim friend. If he does so, both will be surprised and edified by what it says about Christ as the Word of God who took a body like ours, though without sin, and became the son of Mary and the Savior of the world.

The Christian who uses the Qur'an in this way should not fear having to change his religion, since the Qur'an itself tells him, "Let those who follow the Gospel [Christians] judge according to [follow] what God has revealed therein [in the Bible]. Evil-doers are those that do not base their judgements on God's revelations" (Table 5:47, Dawood).

Likewise, any Muslim who has surrendered his life to God will learn that his Qur'an teaches him to love Jesus Christ and to read, study, and follow what is written about Him in the Holy Bible. Here is some of what the Muslim will learn in the Qur'an:

He [an angel] said, "I am but a messenger come from thy Lord, to give thee [Mary] a boy most pure." (Mary 19:19)

He [Christ] said . . . "Blessed He [God] has made me, wherever I may be." (Mary 19:31)

The angels said, "Mary, God gives thee good tidings of a Word from Him whose name is Messiah, Jesus, son of Mary; high honoured shall he be in this world and the next, near stationed to God [nearest to God]." (The House of Imran 3:45)

The Qur'an indicates that followers of Jesus Christ will learn many things about the Holy Bible. For example:

Each one [each believer] believes in God and His Angels, and in His Books and His Messengers; we make no division

[distinction] between any one of His Messengers.
(Cow 2:285)

O believers, believe in God and His Messenger and the
Book He has sent down on His Messenger and the Book
which He sent down before. Whoso disbelieves in God and
His angels and His Books, and His Messengers, and the
Last Day, has surely gone astray into far error. (Women
4:136)

"People of the Book [the Qur'an], you will attain nothing
until you observe [follow] the Torah and the Gospel and
that which is revealed to you from your Lord." (Table 5:68,
Dawood)

What are we to think of Paul's presentation of the gospel to
the Athenians? Instead of quoting from the Bible, he quoted from
literature familiar to the people, literature that came out of "pagan"
traditions. When Paul quoted those words of poetry, he was making not only a cultural connection but a *spiritual* connection as
well. By establishing this common ground with the Athenian
people, he constructed a bridge over which he carried the gospel
message to receptive minds and hearts. Those who consider Paul's
approach carnal and unfruitful should take note of the fact that
Dionysius (a member of the philosophical council that met on that
hill), a woman named Damaris, and several others came to Christ
in response to Paul's message that day, in spite of being at a great
cultural distance from the gospel. These people became the beginning nucleus of the Greek Orthodox Church, which continues to
thrive in the world today.

And so we see with a much broader scope. We see how we
can be more tolerant, tactful, and fruitful in our approach by
respecting the cultures of other people. When we follow this
approach, our testimony is far more likely to be effective in this
culturally and spiritually complex world.

# CHAPTER 3
# A Case for Common Ground

⟨♦⟩

When Paul quoted from a Greek poet as he stood on Mars Hill in Athens, he was not giving a lecture in literature. But he *was* making a key cultural — and spiritual — connection with his audience. This is an approach that is being recognized and used more and more by missionaries throughout the world. And there is solid and consistent support for this approach in the pages of the Bible itself.

Dr. Kenneth Bailey, formerly chairman of the department of New Testament Studies at the Near East School of Theology in Beirut, Lebanon, has a keen grasp of the many cases where biblical writers incorporated nonbiblical literature. Here are two of his main observations:

1. The biblical writers were clearly familiar with the religious and secular literature of their neighbors. Some of this literature, such as the writings of the Babylonian Epics and the Apocrypha, was religious in nature and had considerable respect and authority in the Judeo-Christian community. Other literature was purely secular, much like the Greek poetry Paul quoted to his Athenian audience. The biblical writers from time to time would selectively use terminology and ideas from nonbiblical sources, often

quoting directly. (For example: "Cretans are always liars, evil brutes, lazy gluttons" [Titus 1:12], taken from Epimenides [a Greek prophet]; "See, the Lord is coming with thousands upon thousands of his holy ones to judge everyone . . ." [Jude 14-15], taken from the pseudepigraphal book known as the Assumption of Moses.)

If ancient biblical writers were familiar with such nonbiblical writings—both religious and secular—it stands to reason that Christian Arabs and those living among Muslims should at least have some familiarity with the religious literature that dominates their own cultural setting, especially the Qur'an.

2. Borrowing certain passages of literature to use them in a limited way to illustrate a point does not in any way imply approval of everything in the original literary source. There are at least 133 references or quotations in the New Testament taken from Jewish and Greek nonbiblical literature. The genius of Jesus' use of Jewish literature is seen in His selection of material, His omission of material, and His combination of material. Just because He used ideas and expressions from other sources does not indicate that He approved of everything said by those writers. By the same token, when Christians quote from other books while witnessing, they are by no means stating that everything in them is true or that those books are divinely inspired.

Matthew quoted the Old Testament in much the same way that the rabbis interpreted the Scriptures, which made his approach clearly acceptable to many Jews in his audience. The New Testament writers knew their audience, and God's Spirit enabled them to communicate in familiar thought patterns. Thus, they began in a context familiar to the people when they communicated God's truths.

*

Among modern-day Muslims, God continues to use this method. For example, while I was lecturing in Pakistan, I met a blind believer. "What made you a disciple of Christ?" I asked him.

"The Qur'an," he said.

"How?"

"As I was listening to the Qur'an read on the radio day after day, I heard that Christ was highly honored in this world and the next, and near-stationed to God. I said to myself, 'If I wanted someone to intercede for me to God, who would be better than someone like Christ, who is pure and highly honored and near-stationed to God?' And so I prayed, 'Lord Isa [Jesus], please come to my help. I want to devote myself to God through you. Since you are highly honored and sitting near Him, you can do it.'"

After that, he felt like a changed man, much happier than before. A few days later, a Bible salesman knocked on his door. And so he got a copy of the gospel on cassette. "Where are the people who record this Injeel [the New Testament], and where do they pray together?" the blind man asked the salesman. The salesman gave him the address of the local evangelical church, and the blind man went there and became a member.

This blind man was typical of Muslims in his desire to have someone intercede for him. Muslims actively seek intercession. Most of them believe Muhammad will intercede for them on the Last Day. Since Muhammad's parents died as pagans—unbelievers—he was grieved that God forbade him to intercede for their salvation. The Sunni Muslims believe no one can intercede for anyone else, dead or living, especially not for that person's salvation.

The Qur'an actually forbids interceding for others, except with God's explicit permission: "Who can intercede with Him [God] except by His permission? He knows what is before and behind men. They can grasp only that part of His knowledge which He wills" (Cow 2:255, Dawood).

As we see clearly in the case of this blind man, many passages in the Qur'an have been used effectively alongside the Bible to help Muslims everywhere know exactly who Christ was and how He could help them. This approach using the Qur'an as an entree for Muslims to come to the gospel message has a great deal of common sense behind it. Their attitude about Christ and the Bible is greatly altered when they see that Muhammad spoke so highly in the Qur'an about both of them.

In fact, over and over in the Qur'an, it is stated that if the Jews and the Christians follow faithfully the teaching of their respective books, they will be fine and will not need anything more to be accepted by God: "We sent forth Jesus, the son of Mary, confirming the Torah [Old Testament] already revealed, and gave him the Gospel [New Testament], in which there is guidance and light, corroborating what was revealed before it in the Torah, a guide and an admonition to the righteous" (Table 5:46, Dawood). "But how will they come to you [Muhammad] for judgement, when they already have the Torah which enshrines God's own judgement . . . [and] in which there is guidance and light. By it the prophets who surrendered themselves judged the Jews, and so did the rabbis and the divines. . . . Have no fear of man; fear Me. . . . Unbelievers are those who do not judge [do not put into practice] according to God's revelations" (Table 5:43-44, Dawood). I believe that Muhammad did *not* in any way intend for the Qur'an to be anti-Christ or an anti-Christian document.

Most people living in a Western environment know very little about Muslims and have little interest in learning about Muhammad's life or his intent in Islam. These people may occupy great positions in the world and in the church, but their ignorance of real facts leads them to conclude that Islam and Muhammad should be totally rejected. In some cases these people will point to the Qur'an as a book that is counter to the gospel, not even realizing that the Qur'an itself is largely pro-Christian. This kind of myopia has led to many unnecessarily fruitless debates, strife, and even bloodshed.

Because of the largely pro-Christian attitude in the Qur'an, it seems just as legitimate to use it in our witnessing as to use a pro-Christian quote from any other respected book or leader. God wants us to know His truth. Because of the complexity of cultural circumstances in this world, it is reasonable—indeed, it is a necessity!—that we exercise the same kind of wisdom demonstrated by the writers of the books of the Bible in order to establish common ground with people who otherwise would probably never be open to hearing the gospel message.

# CHAPTER 4
# A Lifestyle That Leads to Life

⟨୨⟩

No farmer would scatter his precious seed on hard soil or pavement and then expect a crop to result. Yet some Christians, with genuine confidence in the power of God's Word but misplaced application, preach it to hardhearted people and then expect it to work like magic.

Jesus told the story of a farmer who decided to spread some seed to grow a crop. Some of the seed that he scattered fell beside a path on unprepared soil. It was devoured by birds. Some of the other seed fell on rocky places. It was withered by the sun. And some of the seed landed among thorns and was choked out. So, in the end none of these seeds bore fruit (Matthew 13:4-7).

Jesus explained that the seed He was referring to in the story was the Word of the kingdom. He said that since those who heard His story weren't prepared to understand it, they were not able to benefit from it. They were like the hard soil along the path. On the contrary, the Devil snatched it away (Matthew 13:19). Not even the Word of God, which is "like a hammer that breaks a rock in pieces" (Jeremiah 23:29) and which is "living and active . . . sharper than any double-edged sword" (Hebrews 4:12), can produce a crop of spiritual results from the soil of an unprepared heart.

But if that seed falls on good soil, which in Jesus' story represents the person who hears the Word of God and has been prepared to understand it, there will be a crop of thirty, sixty, or a hundred times the amount of seed that was originally scattered there (Matthew 13:23).

What, then, is the difference between a responsive and an unresponsive person? One has been prepared to understand and the other hasn't. How do you prepare a person to understand? To understand a totally new idea (which the gospel is to most Muslims), a person must hear it in terms that he understands (that is, from "his own book," from the framework that he has already been exposed to). He must be prepared and open or he will not take the good news of the gospel seriously. He will not *see* it as good news! And if he has always been taught that Christianity is heresy, then he probably won't listen—*unless* that Christian who is in contact with him has become a close, dear friend to him and has a character that commands respect.

Many times people ask me to talk about Christ to a Muslim they know. If the Muslim has not had time to develop a respect for that Christian friend and vice versa, my conversations are almost always futile. But if the Christian has worked on building a close relationship and understanding with his Muslim friend for a good period of time, there will be an immensely different response to what I have to say. The following is a good example of this.

Once when I was in Africa, a Christian woman asked me to visit a Muslim family that she had been befriending for two years. When their car didn't work, she had driven the mother and two children across town to their favorite outdoor vegetable market to shop. Three times they filled her straw basket with fresh vegetables. She carried it to her car each time and dumped it in the trunk, and then drove them back home.

When the other houses in their neighborhood were only getting a trickle of water from their faucets for two weeks, she loaned this family a key to her house so they could come fill their buckets with water and take baths at any time. Some days, only her wet bath mat revealed that three to seven members of that family had bathed in her house. The mother of this family told her landlady, "Not even our own relatives are as good to us as this woman."

When the father moved to Pakistan in an attempt to set up a business with the intent of bringing his family later, the woman allowed them to use her phone to call him long-distance, since they had no phone. They promised to repay her later, but sometimes it was much later and once not at all.

Once, when the mother complained that she suffered from repeated headaches, the Christian woman told her, "In the Bible, Jesus said that if two or three people agree on something and pray about it, God will listen to them" (Matthew 18:19). She then prayed with the mother for God to heal her headaches. The next day the mother told the woman, "My headache is gone, and I took no medicine! Now I'm going to come to you with all my problems." From then on, family members wanted to pray with the woman over every problem. They saw one answer to prayer after another. They had always been religious people and had prayed for years. But they weren't used to seeing answers.

"You pray just the way we do," the mother told the Christian woman. "But God hears your prayers." That opened the door to one of their many conversations about why it is necessary to have Christ to remove our sins in order for a holy God to answer our prayers in His name.

When the woman asked me, "How shall I introduce you to this family?" I said, "Simply as a Christian who loves the Muslims and often reads the Qur'an." They were very excited when she told them this, and they wanted to see me as soon as possible.

As we visited them, it was obvious that the soil had been marvelously prepared. After a long, interesting conversation around the Bible, the Qur'an, and what we were able to glean from them for our present time, they decided to invite us to dinner the following evening, saying they would like to continue the conversation during our meeting the next day.

As we arrived the next evening to a table very generously

covered with all sorts of tasty food and sweets, the father welcomed us very warmly, then said to me, "Whenever our sister, your companion, invites us to a meal in her home, she prays that God would bless the food before we eat it. Will you please do the same this evening?" As we all stood up very reverently and I prayed for God to bless that house, its inhabitants, the food we were going to share together, and all those who love and worship Him sincerely, we all felt like we were one big family, addressing the same heavenly Father, in the name of Christ.

During the long conversation that followed, all the members of the family, without exception, were very friendly, open, and receptive to my witness. I was able to answer all their questions, without any opposition, using verses from the Bible and from the Qur'an, which they very much appreciated.

Soon after I left Africa, I received news that the mother of the family trusted Christ. And to date, three other members of the family have done the same. This is all because our sister had, with great care, prayer, and friendliness, prepared the minds and hearts of these dear people. She did so through her visiting, her caring deeds, offering to share her life, her home, and her personal property with them. And she trusted God to take care of her and the results. The people could not be hostile and resistant to such real love coming from someone they loved and respected on a deep level. Thus God rewarded His servant and honored her faith and trust in Him.

It is so vitally important to prepare the soil of people's hearts if we want to see steady growth and a good harvest. This means not only using a spiritual approach but also a concrete, direct one of kindness, generosity, sharing, and genuine friendliness. And so it is through our consistent, holy lifestyle that we can show others the way to life itself.

# CHAPTER 5
# A Way to View Muhammad and the Qur'an

❦

$S$uppose a man who had shaved off all his hair and who wrapped himself in a bright orange sarong came into my community proclaiming "God's truth." No matter how sincere and loving he was, I would be dead set against renouncing my culture to accept his "truth" about God and becoming like him. But if he behaved according to the ways of my culture and treated my beliefs with respect, it would be far easier to hear what he was saying and to seriously consider it.

Accordingly, we have to attempt to strip our Christianity of the Western cultural forms and trappings with which we have clothed it—*if* we really want Christ to be accepted by the different Muslim peoples of the world. We should give them the liberty to see Christ in forms accepted by their cultures. In some countries—Bangladesh and Yemen, for instance—many Christian workers wear the same garments as the people they are trying to befriend. The Christian women sometimes even veil their faces when going out in public, because this is what God-fearing women do in that culture.

Many people who have trusted Christ in Muslim cultures call themselves "followers of Isa," not "Christians," for the latter has negative cultural implications. Others simply identify themselves as Muslims who are truly surrendered to God through the sacrifice of Messiah Isa (the meaning of *Muslim* is "surrendered"). As is culturally appropriate, the men and women sit separately during worship. Some of them pray with uplifted hands and often with eyes open, as is the habit of the people they are befriending. They chant, not speak, the Lord's Prayer, the attributes of God, and their own testimonies with much animation. They hug one another in typical local fashion, men hugging only men, women hugging only women. They encourage fasting, but clearly teach that it does not earn any special merits with God.

Instead of adopting traditional Christian vocabulary used in the churches of their countries, these followers of Isa employ Muslim terminology. Their places of worship have a loose-knit administrative structure, as mosques do. No foreign money supports this work. Those who are involved pay for the upkeep of the worship place and workers' salaries.

Initially a missionary serves as the teacher, but soon a local follower of Isa takes on this job. To keep the place comfortable to the worshipers, all the Muslims, Hindus, animists, and traditional Christians who visit it are expected to conform to the mode of worship established by that local congregation. As a result, there is no compulsion for those who have trusted Christ to abandon their families. They remain in their homes and maintain a discreet witness. The spiritual fruit of this culturally sensitive approach to worship is great. Most of the growth in these Christian gatherings has resulted from the witness of the new believers who have embraced Christ in this worship-friendly setting. Bible study, prayer, and fasting have made these communities very healthy. In four years one of them saw seventy-five new members come to trust Christ.

By having the freedom to continue practicing many of the familiar exterior forms that local people associate with the worship of God, Muslims feel at home throughout the whole process, even when they come to Christ. They do not feel as if they are accepting a foreign religion or have to forsake their own culture or their family and friends to join these people.

Keeping this cultural sensitivity in mind, it only makes sense that when you are befriending Muslims, it is important not to violate their high regard for Islam and the Qur'an. Even though you may make it quite clear that you love God, if you state reservations about either Islam or the Qur'an you are automatically suspect, and the people will probably not open themselves up to your friendship.

One Christian professor at a Middle Eastern university showed such an ongoing interest in Islam that a Saudi acquaintance asked him, "Do you want to become a Muslim?" The professor, knowing that the word *Muslim* means surrendered to God, said, "I am already a Muslim. I have surrendered to God through Christ." The term and the concept are synonymous. So the Saudi had no reason to close his mind to this professor who referred to passages about Isa—in both the Qur'an and the Bible.

In the seventh century, the Scriptures had not yet been translated into Arabic. Jews and Christians from non-Arab cultures living in Arabia had the Word of God in their languages, but the Arabs did not have Scriptures in Arabic. This is why the Qur'an calls those Arabic people the "common people" (*al ummiyun* in Arabic), meaning, as Muslim commentators have explained, the people whom God did not originally honor by sending them a book of Scriptures in their own language (House of Imran 3:75). The historical perspective of the Arabs is that God remedied this situation by appointing Muhammad to communicate to them in their own language. As the Qur'an says, "It is He [God] who has raised up from among the common people a Messenger [Muhammad] from among them, to recite His signs to them and to purify them, and to teach them the Book and the Wisdom, though before that they were in manifest error" (Congregation 62:2).

It is only when the Arabs received the Qur'an that they were called "the People of the Book," that they were like the other peoples who already had theirs. Muhammad was told by God to say, "'People of the Book, you do not stand on anything, until you perform the Torah and the Gospel, and what was sent down to you from your Lord [the Qur'an].' And what has been sent down to thee from thy Lord will surely increase many of them in insolence and unbelief; so grieve not for the people of the unbelievers" (Table 5:68).

In light of this passage from the Qur'an, it seems that Muhammad saw himself as a "warner" who was bringing the Qur'an in a clear Arabic tongue in order to fill this literary vacuum within the Arab religious culture and to help turn the Arabs from idolatry to worship of the one true God. Indeed, the Qur'an spells out this very perspective: "The unbelievers say of the faithful: 'Had there been any good in it [the Qur'an] they would not have believed in it before us.' And since they reject its guidance, they say: 'This is an ancient falsehood.' Yet before it the Book of Moses was revealed: a guide and a blessing. This Book confirms it. It is revealed in the Arabic tongue, to forewarn the wrongdoers and to give good tidings to the righteous" (The Sand-Dunes 46:11-12, Dawood).

Knowing this historical context helped the professor talk to his students. One day a student visited his office. The student saw him reading a Bible, so he asked him, "Do you believe Muhammad was a prophet?"

If the professor had said no, the student would have immediately lost respect for him, because in his eyes only heretics believed that Muhammad was not a prophet. The professor, knowing that the student was a skeptic, looked out his window at the people a few floors below, walking through town. He said, "If you mean, 'Do I believe that Muhammad is a prophet like those people down there believe it?' then my answer is no. But if you mean, 'Do I believe that he was a prophet like the Qur'an says he was?' then my answer is yes."

The student looked shocked, and said, "What does the Qur'an say?"

The professor answered, "It says he was a warner in a clear Arabic tongue" (see Poets 26:194-195).

The student stood amazed and said, "I've never met anyone like you."

The professor said, "I've never met anyone like you, either."

Thus, the professor kept his student's respect and his own integrity, all because he knew the Qur'an well enough to enable him to avoid treading on his student's beliefs, which certainly would have terminated an open dialogue with him.

Usually when he states his faith to people, this professor freely uses verses from the Qur'an to help them reevaluate their false beliefs about Christ. "If I personally confront them about their erroneous beliefs, who am I?" says the professor. But, on the other hand, he recognizes that if he uses their immense respect for the Qur'an to move them to the point of being willing to study the Bible, then he can maintain a relationship of mutual respect with his Muslim friends at the same time that he presents a more accurate and appealing profile of Jesus Christ.

The fact of the matter is that there are areas of common ground in any culture that can, in some way, be used to help those people be open to God's truth. During the time of Christ, advancing medical arts were of special interest throughout the Roman Empire. So, when Jesus healed people the way He did, He got people's attention in a special way. To many of them, instantaneous and perfect healing meant that Christ could be God, for His healing was so far beyond the rather primitive methods used by the best doctors of that time.

During Muhammad's lifetime in Arabia, literature was highly respected. In fact, it was quite fashionable long before Muhammad's time for the best poems of the famous Arab poets to be displayed on the walls of the Ka'aba, the house of idol worshiping and prayers in Mecca, Saudi Arabia, for all to see.[1]

Muhammad said God revealed the Qur'an to him at the cave of Harra, near Mecca.[2] People considered it a miracle because literature was a form that commanded great respect. To this very day, Muslims across the world hold the highest respect for the literary miracle of the Qur'an.

## Clearing Up Some Misunderstandings

Unfortunately, several myths about Muhammad, Islam, and the Qur'an have pervaded the worldwide Christian community and consequently hindered gospel outreach among Muslims. One myth is that Arabia, the birthplace of Islam, was a desert wasteland populated only by warlike Bedouin tribes who knew nothing about "the one true God," and that Muhammad brought knowledge of this one God, Allah, to these nomadic idol-worshipers. Another myth is that Muhammad was anti-Christian and that his message, the Qur'an, was an anti-Christian book and therefore totally false.

As a result of these myths, Christians throughout the centuries have traditionally believed that Muhammad filled this spiritual vacuum in Arabia with his anti-Christian message, the Qur'an. According to this faulty line of thinking, it would then follow that the Qur'an is totally false and must not be used by Christians in their witness to Muslims. *But* these myths and the resulting erroneous conclusions must be examined using the actual historical facts.

Westerners are wrong to think that the Arabian Peninsula was always populated by Bedouin tribes isolated from the outside world. At the time of Muhammad, there were thousands of Christians and Jews living in Arabia, consisting of many entire tribes. Muhammad respected these Christians and Jews, and was often seen discussing their beliefs with them, both in his hometown of Mecca and along the caravan trade routes. Some of these caravans consisted of up to twenty thousand camels. He was even known to have long talks with the Christian cousin of his wife Khadijah.

Many Jews lived in Arabia, mostly in Medina (a city approximately two hundred miles north of Mecca). In fact, Medina, with an abundance of date palms and goldsmiths, was originally founded by Jews as a commercial city to rival Mecca. There were Jews in Medina who were descended from Babylonian refugees (at the time of Nehemiah and Ezra) and others descended from those who fled the Roman sacking of Jerusalem in A.D. 70. But there were also local native converts to Judaism. Many enterprising Jews did not leave Persia with the Babylonian refugees but were more interested in going where there was money to be made, such as along the caravan routes of the spice trade.

Christianity had been present in the Middle East from the first century A.D. Philip, one of Christ's twelve disciples, gave the gospel to a eunuch who was the Ethiopian minister of finance (Acts 8:26-40). From him, the gospel spread across Ethiopia and the Red Sea to Yemen. In fact, Ethiopia would later defend Yemen in a time of need because they had the same religion.

Consider also the fact that the apostle Paul spent three years in Arabia (Galatians 1:15-18). These efforts resulted in the presence of entire Christian tribes in Arabia. Furthermore, offshoot Christian sects such as the Nestorians sent missionaries throughout Arabia during the sixth and seventh centuries A.D. During this same time period, there was the appearance of Bedouin seekers after the one true God, truly monotheists, who were called "Hanifs." These people were the first to use the term *Allah* for the one God. The term *Allah* comes from *Al-Ilah*, meaning "The God."

Most of Muhammad's knowledge of Christianity and Judaism came from oral discussions and not from written documents. After all, the Bible had not yet been translated into Arabic. Thus Muhammad's knowledge was incomplete. Following long discussions with this curious and intelligent young man, the Jews invited him to come and live with them in Medina. Many of them believed him to be their long-expected Messiah. On September 20, 622 A.D., Muhammad, along with seventy of his followers, entered Medina in a procession where he was treated like a king.

Early chapters from the Qur'an coming from this period were generally quite positive toward both Jews and Christians. Many of these early Qur'anic passages show how much Muhammad respected them. For example, Muhammad appreciated his Christian friends as real worshipers of God and worthy of trust (Table 5:82). He believed they would be saved by God (Table 5:72). He never said Christians were going to hell because they had three gods. In fact, he said he accepted their belief in God (Spider 29:46).

Muhammad was profoundly impressed by the person of Jesus. He called Jesus "the word of God," described His birth and annunciation, described Him as a miracle worker who could raise the dead, who was beloved by God, a messenger, a mercy, and a sign — from God. In fact, Muhammad talked more about Jesus than about any other religious figure. However, later in his ministry, the Jews of Medina rejected Muhammad when they realized he was *not* their Messiah. This parting of the ways was certainly reflected in Muhammad's later Qur'anic chapters, which were harsher in attitude toward Jews.

So, it's important to keep in mind that Arabia was not some kind of wasteland cut off from the outside world, and it was not a spiritual vacuum devoid of knowledge of God. Muhammad did not "bring God" to Arabia. People who believed in "the one God" were already there — in fact, they had been present for almost six centuries. Another thing to keep in mind is that Muhammad was *not* anti-Christian. And although his attitude toward Jews and Christians became more strident in the latter part of the Qur'an, much of the Qur'an is decidedly positive toward Jesus in particular and Christianity in general. These areas of commonality and truth should not be neglected as a bridge to the Muslim heart.[3]

By using the Qur'an, which truly commands a Muslim's highest respect, we are likely to get a positive response from our Muslim friends when we want to emphasize the greatness and uniqueness of Jesus. For instance, let's put together a few passages here:

God's word is the uppermost; God is All-mighty, All-wise. (Repentance 9:40)

When the angels said, "Mary, God gives thee good tidings of a Word from Him whose name is Messiah, Jesus, son of Mary; high honoured shall he be in this world and the next, near stationed to God." (House of Imran 3:45)

When Jesus came with the clear signs he said, "I have come to you with wisdom, and that I may make clear to you some of that whereon you are at variance [you disagree]; so fear you God and obey you me." (Ornaments 43:63)

This last passage here from the Qur'an is of special significance because it shows that Muslims are to obey Jesus. It is easier for a Muslim to listen to Christians speak of Jesus when they quote passages from the Qur'an that emphasize His greatness and uniqueness. It is in large measure not only a matter of honoring Christ but also of showing respect to your Muslim friend.

## A Story of Respect and Sensitivity

Consider the true story of a student who trusted Christ through the influence of loving Christians who treated Islam and the Qur'an with respect. As a result of this relationship of mutual respect and sensitivity, this student was able to remain inside his culture and family.

There was an American Christian who taught at a Middle Eastern university—we'll just call him Tom. A member of a radical Muslim group—we'll call him Hassan—was in the remedial English composition class that Tom taught. Five times a semester he gave his students a short essay to write. One of them was a compare-and-contrast essay. In the list of topics for the essay he put "Islam and Christianity." If a student chose that essay topic and seemed to have an open attitude, Tom would write his usual comments (for example, "good sentence structure") at the end of the essay, and then he would add, "Maybe we could get together and discuss this, if you are interested." Hassan responded to such a note.

Tom went through a few of "The Seven Muslim-Christian Principles" (covered later in this book) with him. Hassan genuinely enjoyed what he was discovering.

As he got to know Tom and his friends, they invited him to a meeting for students who were close to trusting Christ or who had already done so. There the Qur'an was quoted, and the Bible was used at length, especially the Gospel of Matthew. Hassan met some Muslim students who had trusted Christ. He noticed that they talked about being "in the kingdom of God" rather than referring to their change as joining a religion. Emotional labels like "Christian," "church," and "baptism" were avoided, since they were considered politically loaded terms. They never talked about "changing religious allegiance" because in their culture that meant to become a churchgoer, and to break with their culture, people, and family.

After that initial positive exposure, different people whom Hassan had met at the meeting would read the Bible with him. One would stop by his house two or three times a week, discussing it and praying with him. Hassan came to love the Bible. He would read the Gospels when he was by himself.

Hassan was the oldest son in his family—a highly honored and privileged position. His younger brothers didn't like what he was doing, and although a younger brother was never supposed to berate the oldest one, one younger brother did, saying, "You are corrupting yourself with such a corrupt book and such corrupt friends."

Hassan replied, "Let me ask you a question: If a Christian said something against the prophet Muhammad to you, what would you do?"

The brother replied, "I would beat him to death."

"And if you said something against Jesus to a Christian, what would he do?"

His brother replied, "He would forgive me."

Hassan said, "Which one lacks love and respect? And which one is not able to hold his wrath because he is corrupt?"

The younger brother ran to his father, saying, "Hassan is trying to convert me."

Hassan said, "I am not trying to convert you. You have eyes. You can see."

In the course of a few years of exposure to the Bible and believers, Hassan trusted Christ. But numerous temptations nearly kept him from truly following Him. For example, he intended to marry a certain woman whose thinking he assumed he could change. Their relationship was on and off again and again. It was a physically pure relationship, but he saw her often, which in Arab culture declared his intent to marry her. If he didn't, this would bring unbelievable shame, especially to her — and an Arab avoids shame at all costs.

Hassan would pray about it with a Christian doctor friend because he felt God did not want him to see her. The doctor agreed. But the next day Hassan would be in the back of the library talking with her again. For months Hassan wavered between his decision not to see her and his desire for her. His interest in the Bible faded. He only read it once a month, when he associated with other believers.

One day Hassan came to see the doctor and the Arab believers the doctor lived with. They were huddled around a gas lamp because there was no electricity due to bombing. Puffing on a cigarette wrapped in corn husks, he announced in a cloud with a foul odor that he was finished with her. No one said a word, which meant, in Arab culture, that they didn't think he would follow through with his decision. He swore that he would never see her again. The doctor asked, "Why are you so sure?"

Hassan replied, "I see that she intends to change me, and we cannot walk together." And so he narrowly escaped marrying a woman who could have made his life bitter.

"I have another question," said Hassan to these men who had prayed and prayed for him. "I am enjoying reading the Qur'an more than the Bible. The Bible does not make sense in a lot of things."

"Tell me more," said the doctor. "Of course, it is natural you would feel comfortable reading the Qur'an. You were raised on it."

"Which one should I continue reading?" Hassan asked.

"It's up to you," said the doctor. "As far as I am concerned, you should read both of them."

"But you cannot read both of them together," said Hassan. "You cannot carry those two in one hand. So which one should I drop?"

"You need to read both of them," said the doctor, careful not to give him any directive advice.

"I cannot."

"Then read them both until the books themselves tell you which one to read," said the doctor.

"I thought that is what you would say," said Hassan, smiling.

After that, Hassan developed a greater hunger for the Bible, reading it all the time.

Because Hassan loved the Bible and chose to read it (no one told him that he had to), he continues to read it, even with his friends from the same radical political group he belonged to previous to his pursuit of Christ. These friends would never have done that before. Hassan now has a contact who supplies him with New Testaments. In his friends' rooms at the university he can tell if they've been reading their Bibles if the pages are slightly soiled by their fingers. But he doesn't push those who haven't been reading.

Hassan has by no means become an established and mature follower of Christ. He still has a violent temper. But he loves the Bible and loves sharing it with these people who are untouchable by others outside his radical group. He loves Christ and is associated with at least one of the thirty groups that are sharing the Bible among their friends and neighbors in that country.

This is an ongoing story, one that Satan is eager to terminate. Since you have read it, it is important for you to pray, for this is a serious spiritual battle.

1. See Thomas Wright, *Christianity in Arabia* (London: Leicester Square), p. 106.

2. See Ibn Saad, *AT-Tabaqat El-Qobra* (Beirut: Sadar Press), 1:194.

3. For more information about the historical background of Muhammad and his early exposure to Jews and Christians, see John B. Christopher, *The Islamic Tradition* (New York: Harper & Row, 1972), pp. 6-15; W. Montgomery Watt, *Mohammed: Prophet and Statesman* (Oxford: Oxford University Press, 1961), pp. 6,40; Robert Payne, *The History of Islam* (New York: Dorset Press, 1959), pp. 23-32,80.

# CHAPTER 6
# A Balanced Approach

❦

M any areas of sensitivity are required when we try to meet Muslims and build bridges between the Muslim and Christian communities. There is often much at stake. On one hand, we need to consider the chance of death threats, endangered lives, or being disowned by family and culture. On the other hand, there is the discovery of new spiritual life through faith. But we are not likely to advance in this enterprise unless we are willing to use the Qur'an to move a person toward using the Bible so that he can find living truth in Christ. But there must be a well-thought-out, balanced strategy to this whole process.

✳

One day, a lady doctor at the mission hospital in a Middle Eastern city where I lived called me on the telephone and told me she had a patient who wanted to commit suicide. The doctors had tried everything medically and psychologically that they could think of, but nothing helped. So the doctor asked me to come see her.

I entered her room, and there I found a beautiful young woman in her mid-twenties, sitting on the edge of her bed, weeping desperately.

"Can I help you?" I asked her.

"No one can help me," she said.

"What are you going to do if no one can help you?" I asked.

"I will end my life," she said.

"What will happen to you after that?" I asked.

"What do you mean?" she asked.

"Aren't you a Muslim? You should know about these things," I said.

"Even when you are a Muslim, you do not think of those things," she answered.

"Maybe I can help you, or bring someone to help you," I said. She burst into tears. I prayed in my heart for the Lord to show me how to help her while I waited for her to calm down.

"You look like a good man," she said. "I will tell you my story. I am the oldest of five children. Our well-to-do father divorced our mother and gave us one room in the house to live in. My mother works a little. My three sisters are in school. My brother is a young soldier in the army, but he won't help us financially. So I work in the morning in a bank and in the evening as a TV announcer to support six people.

"My father recently brought another woman into the house. They want us to leave so there will be room for her grown-up sons. Since we haven't left, they throw stones and dirt at us and curse us. So why should I live? It's better to die since no one can help us."

"That's true," I said. "You can't expect any help from this world. But I'm sure you must have heard this: 'Come to me, all you who are weary and burdened'" (Matthew 11:28).

"No," she said. "Who said that?" I opened my New Testament and read that passage.

"What is that book?" she asked.

"It is the Injeel," I said. *Injeel* is the Qur'an's word for New Testament.

"Oh, then it is the Lord Christ," she said.

"Do you love Him?" I asked.

"He is one of our prophets," she said.

"He is my Lord, and I have been living with Him all these years, and He has never failed me in all my troubles and all my needs," I said.

"How is that?" she asked. So I told her how Christ saved me when I was in a desperate state of a life of sin. Her face revealed that she was interested.

"If you trust in Him, He will do the same for you," I concluded.

"I know that He does miracles," she said, "but I do not think He can do a miracle for me."

"You do not know because you have not tried Him," I explained. "Would you promise me one thing?"

"What?" she asked.

"Keep quiet tonight, and I will come tomorrow to talk more about this." I wanted her to calm down and to think about what I had said. "I will leave this part of the Injeel with you. And, if it is all right with you, I will pray for Christ to help you and send my wife to bring you a complete Holy Injeel. And tomorrow we will see what Christ has inspired you to do. But promise me that you will not do anything to yourself until tomorrow." She promised.

I read her all of Matthew 11, insisting on its final part, and prayed out loud for the Lord to provide a way out of her dilemma. Later that day my wife brought her an Arabic New Testament and Psalms (Zabur) and read Psalm 23 to her. "You are a sheep of the Lord, and He will take care of you," my wife told her, and prayed with her, too.

Three or four hours later the lady doctor called me back. "What did you do to the young woman?" she said, dropping the formality of calling me by my usual title of "Pastor."

"Did she jump out of the window?" I asked.

"No," said the doctor. "She got up, washed her face, paid her bill, thanked us, and left."

"Give me her address and phone number," I asked. And so, we were able to contact her and invite her to dinner at our house. "Are you better?" I asked her when she came.

"I want to know more about our Lord Christ," she said. That night she put her trust in Christ. She visited us often. "Everyone in the bank says that I have changed completely," she told us. "They ask then, 'Who changed you?' I say, 'Our Lord Christ came to my heart and changed me.' They ask, 'Oh, you have become a Christian?' I say, 'No. I am a Muslim. Our Lord Christ is for everyone.'"

She didn't mention her problems at home anymore. She brought her sisters one after the other to our house until they also had put their trust in Christ. The four of them would eat dinner with us. We would read the Bible together and pray and sing.

Once, on Good Friday, she came to visit us unexpectedly. "We are sorry that we cannot stay and visit with you. We are going to church," we told her.

"Oh, please take me with you."

At church, she took Communion with us. Afterwards, the pastors interrogated me about whether she was baptized or not. "Where in the Bible does it say you have to be baptized to take Communion?" I asked them. Later on I heard that they had written the church leaders about it, but nothing further came of the matter.

I had no intention to tell her about baptism. She had the Holy Spirit living inside her and the Bible to tell her what to do. If I had insisted that she leave the mosque and become a nominal Christian by coming to church and being baptized, she would have been cut off from her family, her people, and her culture, and totally unable to be salt and light to them (Matthew 5:13-16).

## Treading Softly

In many Muslim countries, death is a real possibility for someone who blatantly broadcasts the fact that he or she is a Christian. The following story bears this out.

I once addressed a group of professors and friends at a missionary school in the Middle East. While I was speaking, Jamil, a Christian Arab professor of English, stood up and interrupted me.

"I cannot stand it anymore. Something is burning in my heart." I had been telling the story of the man who asked Jesus to cure his sick son and was told, "Everything is possible for him who believes" (Mark 9:17-27).

"Keep quiet and continue praying until I finish my talk," I told him. He knelt down and prayed silently right there in the middle of the meeting. After I finished, I asked him what he wanted to say. He answered, "I am supposed to be a godly man, since I am a Bible teacher here in my school. But I want to receive a new, holy life this minute. I have been a hypocrite all these years. It's as if I'm seeing Christ face-to-face right now." And he wept.

After putting his trust in Christ that day, he brought his students to talk with me about the gospel from time to time. He even went out in the streets, distributing Bibles in various places. This is unheard of for a professor from a well-known school. As he became bolder, his life was threatened, for it became known that he was leading Arabs to Christ. He knew the full implications of what those threats meant, but he didn't care.

On teachers' day, when students brought presents to their teachers, a student told him, "There are some people outside who want to see you." He went out, and they kidnapped him. The school and the police searched for him, but did not find him. A few days later, Jamil's body was found. They had tied a stick of dynamite around his neck and blown him to pieces. His sister found some of his skin with a birthmark on it, and confirmed that it was his body.

A different professor in a different country took a totally different approach. He took the threat on his life seriously, and lived. He was the assistant director of a well-known university in the Middle East. But his happiness in teaching was eventually marred by his daughter's illness. She was his only daughter and he was so very fond of her, but no physicians there could cure her. He sent her for advanced treatment in England, where she rented a room in the home of a Christian family. The doctors were having a difficult time because her case was so complicated. The Christian family she lived with told her that Christ was a healer, so she prayed together with them and also by herself that He would heal her.

Meanwhile, her father was at home, worrying about her. One night Christ appeared to him in a dream. The professor asked Him, "What do You want from me, Lord Isa?"

"I do not want anything from you," said Christ. "I am bringing you good news. I am going to heal your daughter. And I hope you don't forget what I do for her." The man woke up, perplexed.

While he was eating his breakfast that morning, his daughter called from London. "Daddy! Daddy! I am healed! I am all right now!" she exclaimed.

"Yes, I know," he said, with a sense of wonder in his voice.

"Who told you?" she asked with astonishment.

"The One who healed you came to me at night in a dream and told me. I have promised Him to be grateful for this. So now I must figure out what to do."

He went to see the ruler of their country, a good friend of his, to tell him the story. When he told him what had happened, the statesman replied, "This is very good. I know that Christ is visiting our nation these days!"

"Are we going to do something about it?" the professor asked.

"Like what?"

"We have to broadcast it on television and everywhere," the professor said.

"What are you saying? Do you want the fanatics to liquidate us?" he said with fear in his eyes.

"Then what shall we do?" asked the professor.

"Tell no one, and live as if nothing has happened," said the ruler.

"That *might* be a wise thing to do," said the professor. But the fire in his heart made him reconsider. He began to talk about his experience openly. One day a student of his came to see him and pulled out a revolver. But his hand was shaking and the professor was able to knock it out of his hand, and the student ran away.

Then it became clear to the professor that although this boy was not able to kill him, the next one might. So he left the country, took his daughter with him, and moved to Europe. A few years later the statesman whom the professor had visited was, ironically enough, assassinated by the fanatics he had feared so much.

The point here is that we must tread softly. Most people are not yet as ripe as the young woman I met in the hospital. So you have to go slowly from the very beginning. This work is usually accomplished only through a process of friendship, prayer, and fasting. After a long friendship that has given your friend confidence in you, then you might be able to say, "I would like to know more about your Qur'an and your religion. Perhaps you would like to know more about the Bible and my Christianity. Let us come together to learn from each other about our respective beliefs."

## Developing the Relationship

It is good to start with what you have in common, like Christ's miracles, the Virgin Birth, etc. Then you can slowly proceed to the fact that Christ was a prophet, then to the kind of prophet He was. (Examples of Christ's miracles can be found in Table 5:110 in the Qur'an, and in Matthew 8:1-34, Matthew 12:22-45, and John 9:1-41 in the Bible. Examples of the Virgin Birth can be found in Mary 19:16-22 in the Qur'an, and Matthew 1:18-23 and Luke 1:26-35 in the Bible.)

Or you can start with a group of people you have befriended. Talk about some things the Qur'an says that you also believe. Although this wouldn't be the kind of thing that could be pursued very far in a group setting, someone who is interested might later come to you alone with his questions. Meet him as often as he wants to. Drink coffee together. Converse with him. Extend your time with him as much as possible. This heightens the friendship. Friendship backed by prayer is the most important dimension of developing a dialogue with a Muslim.

I have divided the content of what you can share in that kind of friendship dialogue into seven principles, which I explain in chapters 9 to 15. You don't have to present these principles exactly as they are laid out here. But you'll want to be sure that your friend thoroughly understands the concepts of one principle before you proceed to the next. Freely discuss the points of each principle for as long as he wants to, but don't bore him with more than he wants. Read the references from the Qur'an and the Bible out loud. This will allow you and your friend to get used to each other's Book, especially if you read from his and he reads from yours.

One of the foundation stones of Samuel Zwemer's ministry was that he wanted Muslims to understand there is another way. This concept does not translate well to a Muslim, however, because a Muslim says there is only one way, God's way. If you advocate anything else, that's blasphemy. This is all the more reason why you have to go side by side with a Muslim, communicating with him through his own religious book, in his way. You use his book and his way of thinking to let him see that you are more on his side than he is. In this method of sharing, you get to choose, from the framework of your own beliefs, what you think will communicate best to him. As you do so, you must always be sensitive in the timing and manner you use to reveal it to him.

I have followed Dr. Zwemer's ministry for quite a long period. Although it's been years since his death, I still observe in Arabia, the Arabian Gulf region, Qatar, and Oman the profound results of his ministry. His spiritual legacy goes on. I am astounded at the zeal of the people I visit in those places who were touched by Dr. Zwemer through his visits there. He established many friendly relationships, and left a number of Arabic Bibles, which are still passed from fathers to sons. He prepared the fields and the hearts, sowing in them the good seed, and I personally have been able, through the years, to joyfully reap quite a harvest from that spiritual work he started.

Typically Christians and Muslims look to their respective *beliefs* as perfectly true and consider their *system of logic* completely sound. Yet some teachings seem to contradict other teachings, so what do we do in those situations? In many cases we must acknowledge that certain truths are far beyond our understanding. For example, the *Creation* is an indisputable fact. We are surrounded by it, able to touch it, see it, live with it, and describe it in great detail. The *Creator*, on the other hand, is unseen, untouchable, and most of His attributes and prerogatives cannot be easily defined. Yet one cannot accept the first and exclude the other. Both of them are perfectly true.

The Bible and the Qur'an express the idea that at certain moments of the day or the night, the sun and the moon rise up or sit down. This, in fact, appears to be a blatant scientific error, since we know that it is not the sun rising but the earth turning. But were the writers in this case really trying to state a scientific fact or to express a poetic image? Obviously the latter. And so we must not create a problem where there is none.

Or, consider some of the descriptions of God in both the Qur'an and the Bible: "Whatever good you expend is for yourselves, for then you are expending, being desirous only of God's Face" (Cow 2:272). "The eyes of the LORD are on those who fear him, on those whose hope is in his unfailing love" (Psalm 33:18). "[God] must reign until he has put all his enemies under his feet" (1 Corinthians 15:25).

The questions that should come to our minds in reading these references are: Does God really have a face, eyes, feet, etc.? Or, are these figurative expressions used to give us at least a hint about this great God who is really impossible for us to understand with our puny minds? We also use expressions like "the rising sun" or "God's face" so that we may understand and relate to each other.

One of the subjects that is a cause of continuous controversy between the faithful of these two peoples, Muslims and Christians, is the matter of Christ's "Sonship." If a Christian quotes John 3:16 to a Muslim—"God so loved the world that he gave his one and only Son, that whoever believes in him shall not perish but have eternal life"—the Muslim will say immediately, "What? God marrying and having a son?! You are worse than an unbeliever to believe this." And if we have not carefully read and understood all the preceding text in John, we may indeed be guilty of what the

Muslim accuses us of. But in light of the biblical context whenever Christ is referred to as God's Son, we should understand that the word "Son" is not being used in a physical sense. In fact, it is often used in the Bible and the Qur'an in other than a physical sense.

First, let's look at the Bible. Jesus gave His disciples James and John, who were brothers, the nickname "Sons of Thunder" (Mark 3:17). We see also in Scripture that the early Christians named Joseph, a Levite from Cyprus, Barnabas, which meant "Son of Encouragement" (Acts 4:36). King Lemuel called his son "son of my womb" and "son of my vows" (Proverbs 31:2). We see the same kind of thing in the Qur'an. The traveler who is in need of assistance and help is called "son of the road" (some examples: Cow 2:177,215; Women 4:36; Spoils 8:41).

A related Christian doctrine that is considered blasphemous by Muslims is the Trinity. And yet the Muslim condemnation of this doctrine has been based on certain false assumptions:

1. One false assumption is that a man (referring to Jesus Christ), who possesses a created body, cannot be associated ontologically (in terms of personal being) with the Godhead. "God has said: You shall not serve two gods, for He is but one God. Fear none but Me" (Bee 16:51, Dawood).

2. Another false assumption is that, according to Christian teaching, a woman, a virgin named Mary, has sex with God and bears a son, thus she comes to be known as "the Mother of God," which is a concept found in heathen mythology: "And when God said, 'O Jesus son of Mary, didst thou say unto men, "Take me and my mother as gods, apart from God"?' He said, 'To Thee be glory! It is not mine to say what I have no right to. If I indeed said it, Thou knowest it'" (Table 5:119).

3. A third false assumption is that the concept behind the Trinity was associated in some way with the blasphemous claims of some of the angels known as

jinn, who rebelled against God and pretended that they were equals to Him. "They ascribe to God, as associates, the jinn, though He created them; and they impute to Him sons and daughters without any knowledge. Glory be to Him!" (Cattle 6:100). Also: "When We said to the angels: 'Prostrate yourselves before Adam,' all prostrated themselves except Satan [Iblis], who was a jinnee [evil angel] disobedient to his Lord. Would you then serve him and his offspring as your masters rather than Myself, despite their enmity towards you? A sad substitute the wrongdoers have chosen!!" (Cave 18:50, Dawood).

These are false assumptions that many Muslims make based on an incomplete understanding of Christian doctrine and of the Qur'an itself. But the following passages from the Qur'an seem to indicate that Muhammad was quite open to the Christian doctrines of the Virgin Birth, the Trinity, and the Sonship of Jesus Christ.

Dispute not with the People of the Book [Jews and Christians] save in the fairer manner, except for those of them that do wrong; and say, "We believe in what has been sent down to us, and what has been sent down to you; our God and your God is One." (Spider 29:46)

Say you, "We believe in God, and in that which has been sent down on us and sent down on Abraham, Ishmael, Isaac and Jacob, and the Tribes, and that which was given to Moses and Jesus and the Prophets, of their Lord: we make no division between any of them, and to Him we surrender." (Cow 2:136)

The Messenger believes in what was sent down to him from his Lord, and the believers; each one believes in God and His angels, and in His Books and His Messengers; we

make no division between any one of His Messengers.
(Cow 2:285)

When Muhammad confronted Christians about having three gods, he was not attacking the idea of the Father, Son, and Holy Spirit in the Godhead. He was attacking the idea of God having a wife and then having a son by her (see Table 5:116 and Jinn 72:3). Otherwise, it is impossible to explain what the Qur'an says in this specific language: "Dispute not with the People of the Book [Jews and Christians] save in the fairer manner, except for those of them that do wrong; and say, 'We believe in what has been sent down to us, and what has been sent down to you; our God and your God is One'" (Spider 29:46). The Qur'an thus affirms that the Christian God is the true God. Since Muhammad knew the Christians' belief concerning a Trinitarian God, this verse would make no sense if Muhammad were attacking the Trinity.

The Muslim thinks his beliefs are the most cohesive in all religions. He is deeply convinced of his system of logic. It is not logical to him that God would have a son. A Christian obviously has a different understanding of Father and Son. This is a case in which the Muslim mind believes one thing and will usually not consider what seems to conflict with it. Thus a Christian must exercise sensitivity and respect at this point in the dialogue.

Muslims think Christians believe that God had sex with Mary. They don't have a problem with the Virgin Birth (see Prophets 21:91 and Forbidding 66:12). But they think some Christians don't really believe it!

To keep from losing your chance to interest your friend, give a brief answer to any question he has about the Sonship of Christ until he comes to really know Him. For example, you could explain that in the Qur'an it talks about "the son of the road" (Cow 2:177,215). Ask him, "Can a road marry and have sons?" Of course not. Or about where it mentions God sitting on his throne (Ta Ha 20:5): "Can God really sit and stand?" Again, no. These are figurative expressions God uses to help us understand. It is exactly like when the Bible tells us, "the sun rose," or, "the sun set," when we know perfectly well that the sun does not rise or set but that the earth's rotation makes it appear so. God uses these expressions so that we will understand through metaphor and analogy.

Later on in your relationship with your Muslim friend, you could mention the story of Gabriel appearing to Mary to tell her of her virgin pregnancy. This might help him see the logic of Christ submitting and serving in the role of Son as a sacrificial act, and thus the logic of the title Son of God. But this should be well on into your relationship with him, because many Muslims have a harsh emotional reaction to the phrase "Son of God." Initially, questions on the topic can be postponed with "I'll answer you in more detail when we study that later."

Some of you may object to this method, saying it is deceptive and does not teach the whole truth. But remember that the teaching does not stop here. He will come to grasp Christ's Sonship after he gets to know Christ, since then he will have a fuller picture of the Scriptures and also the Holy Spirit's enlightenment. "Do not make the oven too hot or else you will burn the meat" (that is, don't overdo it) and lose your friend before you even have a chance to help him find the truth about Christ.

## Using the Qur'an

Knowing many relevant parts of the Qur'an can significantly heighten your ability to deal with opposition and explain the gospel. Once, for example, when I was entering a certain Middle Eastern country, a customs official wanted to confiscate my Bible. I asked him why, and he said, "Because it is forbidden."

"Why?" I asked.

"Because it talks so much about Israel," he replied.

"Are you a Muslim or a Christian?" I asked.

"Why do you ask?" he said.

"Because I want to know where you get your ideas," I said.

"A Muslim, of course."

"Don't you read the Qur'an?" I asked him. The man felt

insulted. I took a Qur'an from my pocket and showed him what it said about Israel and the Bible. The official then agreed to let the Bible enter his country. But he had to save face somehow. Well, since in ancient times maps did not appear in the back of Bibles, the official said the maps had to go. So we cut all the maps out of the Bible with a razor blade.

Before you start quoting verses from the Qur'an, make sure you understand them clearly. Don't count on your Muslim friend grasping your points right away. They will have no impact if their meaning is not clear to him. A little repetition can help drive your points home.

If your friend knows Arabic, you can have him read the verse from the Qur'an in Arabic and tell you what it means. And if you have done your homework, you can also help him see relevant verses from the Bible.

But if you are using a translation of the Qur'an, it is not so easy. Most translations of the Qur'an add traditional Muslim interpretations, injecting what Muslim scholars have taught over the years. Some verses about Christ and the Bible are changed to the point of meaning something totally different from the original Arabic of the Qur'an. One example of this is the English translation of the Arabic particle *innama* in the Qur'an. It is accurately translated "The believers indeed are brothers" (see Apartments 49:10). But it is wrongly altered in the following quotation: "The Messiah, Jesus son of Mary, was only the Messenger of God, and His Word that He committed to Mary, and a Spirit from Him" (Women 4:171). This translation carries an interpretation that reflects inconsistency with many other passages from the Qur'an when it implies that Christ is not also the Word of God, a Spirit from Him, sinless, high-honored in this world and the next, sitting near God, etc.

I consider the most accurate English translation of the Qur'an to be the one by Arthur J. Arberry, a non-Muslim.[1] But Arberry falls into the same kind of interpretative errors I just described, even though he was scholarly in his approach. One drawback of this translation is that it is largely written in Shakespearean English.

Using the Qur'an successfully hinges on being able to show that its real intention was pro-Bible, pro-Christ, and pro-Christian, as we will see more and more in our approach. A biased translation/interpretation of the Qur'an will only obscure this and be much less useful.

A few minor precautions will protect you from offending your friend's sense of the sanctity and superiority of the Qur'an. First, you may not want to have the verses from the Qur'an and those from the Bible on the same sheet of paper. Second, don't go to him with a printed page of what you want to discuss with him. That would seem as if you had a certain agenda to force on him, and he will react negatively.

Also, beware of the words "evangelism," "missions," and "convert." These are all emotionally charged words. Instead of "evangelism," use more loving terms like "sharing," "discussing," or "having a mutual exchange of ideas." The word "evangelism" implies that I am right and you are wrong, and that kind of exchange just doesn't do much good.

If you use the word "missions" with your friend, he thinks of the Crusades of the eleventh to the thirteenth centuries and the atrocities committed then. "Missions" is a political term and has other negative connotations, too. "Convert" is not a good term to use, either, when talking about those who have trusted Christ. To those who have *not* trusted Christ, this word implies not only betraying one's religion but also one's own people, family, and culture. When your friend comes into a vital relationship with Jesus Christ, you could use terms such as "truly surrendered to God through Jesus Christ" or "believer in Jesus Christ" or just "believer."

Also, it may be wise to wait to show your Muslim friend the Qur'an's verses upholding the validity of the Bible as long as possible in your relationship with him. It is his deeply ingrained belief that the Qur'an is the only holy book. After you have won his confidence as a friend and as a God-fearing person, and after he has come to have a hunger to know more about Christ and to read the Bible, then he is ready to see these verses that contradict a long-cherished belief. Always keep in mind that it is best not to move toward one extreme or another. Have a balanced strategy that you have spent a lot of time researching, thinking about, and praying about.

But to effectively bring your friend into a deep relationship with Christ, you cannot just learn a technique. You have to put yourself in his shoes. Few of us can make that step. He needs to smell the fragrance of Christ on you. He will also be able to smell whether or not you really love him or if you are secretly condemning and criticizing him. He has a strong sense of smell in this respect. Westerners talk to each other to explain. Easterners do not talk a lot, and yet they gather much information without talking. We all know that a person has five senses to perceive things. But I think we all have a sixth sense that tells us about another person's attitude about us.

But even if your approach is flawless and your sensitivity to your friend's open nerves is finely tuned, remember that although what you have embarked on is not easy, it could bring a whole new spiritual richness into your life. You may often think that this relationship will never go anywhere, and you may feel like giving up. But Jesus' response to His disciples was, "With man this is impossible, but with God all things are possible" (Matthew 19:26).

---

1. A. J. Arberry, trans., *The Koran Interpreted* (New York: Macmillan, Collier Books, 1955).

# CHAPTER 7
# Be Shrewd and Innocent

ॐ

The moment you become confident that you really understand how to relate the truth of Christ to Muslims, watch out. It is one thing to be calm, respectful, and culturally sensitive. It is quite another to be casual and indiscreet in your presentation of the gospel. You need to be aware of potential barriers and pitfalls, even things that may threaten your life. So let's take a look at some areas where we need to be vigilant. This is more than just a matter of the right protocol. It is a matter of potential danger. In this case, to "beware" means to "be aware."

When Jesus sent His disciples out on their own to proclaim the gospel, this is one of the things He told them: "I am sending you out like sheep among wolves. Therefore be as shrewd as snakes and as innocent as doves" (Matthew 10:16). Muslims cannot take offense at the reference to "wolves" in this passage, for the fact is that at this particular time Jesus was sending His disciples just to the Jews. But there are extremists and hateful people in *any* culture. So the Lord's warning here applies to all witnessing ventures. Be shrewd — without sacrificing your innocence. Be holy, but also be wise.

Recently some Bengalis from Bangladesh and Tamils from

India were expelled from several European countries under the pretext that they had entered those countries illegally and that some were involved in selling drugs. The majority of them protested that these expulsion decisions were biased, based on prejudiced ideas about their religious and political views.

Likewise, when some Christians were recently expelled from an Arab country, a good Muslim in a high position said, "These people are following their religion. We call ourselves religious people. Why are we expelling them? If their belief is from God, He will cause it to prosper. If not, He will cause it to end."

But the political authorities said, "Out!" In other words, they were not much interested in doing what was godly. Politics dictates action. It's not a simple, clear-cut issue of religion, but politics and ethnic prejudice muddy the waters when it comes to how Christians are received in Muslim countries—and vice versa. The sad reality is that such ethnic prejudice runs contrary to the teachings of the Bible and the Qur'an. Although a strong distinction is made between religion and the government in "Christian nations," Islamic nations have not reached that point. They are religious and political at the same time. But in *all* nations, there is ethnic prejudice.

It is good to be aware of these complex realities so that you can understand where your friends are coming from, what they think, why this deep rift separates us, and how to try to remedy it. There are so very many problems to deal with.

Around fifteen years ago, one of our children was working in a carpet factory in the Middle East. One day a young man came to me with an Arabic Bible in his hand and said, "I work with your son, and he has sent me to you so you can help me understand some of the difficult passages I am finding in reading this book."

"Oh, yes," I said. "But why didn't my son explain them to you? He knows the Bible as well as I do."

"It's a long story," the man replied, "but let me tell you briefly. A few months ago I needed a job, so I went to the owner of a carpet factory and asked him if he had a job opening for me in his factory. He told me, 'Our manager, Mr. Antony, will see if you are needed and can work for us. Go see him. He's over there.'

"I said to myself," continued the man, "'Antony is a Christian name. I know how arrogant and ungodly these Christian people are with us.' But since I needed to find work very badly, I thought, 'Let me try it for a while and if it doesn't work out, it will at least allow me to have the time to find something else.'

"So I went to Antony. He received me very kindly, even offering me a cup of coffee, and immediately hired me to work in the factory. I started working, but watched him out the side of my eye, waiting for him to start persecuting me and ill-treating me. I was astonished to find him so kind with everybody. He was never angry or bad-tempered, and never swore or cursed. He never came to work half-drunk or spent all day smoking, as other Christians habitually do in my country. On the contrary, he always spoke softly and politely with people. All this made me doubt whether he could be a Christian.

"Curious to know exactly what he was, I went up to him one day and asked, 'Antony, may I ask you what your religion is?' 'I am a Christian,' he replied. 'But why do you ask?' When I explained the whole story, he laughed and said, 'I am a different Christian. I constantly read the Bible.' I asked him what the Bible was, and when he explained it to me, I told him that I would like to read it. And he brought me one. So I started to read the Bible, and the more I read, the more I felt I wanted to read it. But of course, I had some difficulty fully understanding everything. When this happened, I went to Antony to get him to explain it to me, which he always kindly did, until I began taking too much of his time at the factory.

"He called me one day and said, 'Listen, my friend. If you want somebody who has more time and can explain to you better than I, here is my father's address. Go see him in your free time, with my blessing.' This is why I have come to see you." As he finished his story, he smiled broadly.

## Muhammad's So-Called Illiteracy

There are certain problems that occur between Muslims and Christians that seem insurmountable. There are many reasons why Muslims consider the Qur'an to be a miracle. One of them is, How could Muhammad, an illiterate man, have produced it? However, the facts written about Muhammad in the Qur'an, his biography, and other sources reveal that he may not have been illiterate. Let us consider some of these facts.

Muhammad's father died before he was born. His mother died when he was six. After that, his grandfather set out to raise him. But two years later, when his grandfather was dying, the old man made his son, Abu Talib, Muhammad's uncle, promise to treat the boy with as much care as he would his own sons. The uncle swore to do this. In traditional Arab culture, a man's word carries incredible weight. It is considered utterly reliable. So after the death of his grandfather, Muhammad went to live with his uncle's family.

Ali, one of the uncle's children, was one of the most learned, educated Arabs of his time. Yet some say that Muhammad was illiterate. This would imply that the uncle had gone back on what he swore to his father about Muhammad. How could Muhammad have been illiterate if his cousin Ali was so learned? We find that the Qur'an itself resolves this supposed discrepancy for us.

In the Qur'an, Muhammad is called the *ummi* prophet. Some Muslims have taken the word *ummi* to mean that he could not read or write. But this word can also mean "who is not of those who read the Scriptures," or "Gentile" (see Pickthall's note at Heights 7:158[1]). When you put this together with the facts regarding Ali's education, Muhammad's uncle's oath, and the reliability of an Arab's word, is there another possible meaning? Yes. In many places the Qur'an refers to "the People of the Book" (that is, people who have Scriptures) as opposed to the *ummiyoun*, the plural of *ummi*. Most Muslim commentators say that *ummiyoun* means people who do not have a divine book, that is, people who are illiterate regarding the Scriptures but not illiterate *per se*.

## Points Frequently Considered Contradictions
## in the Qur'an

Muhammad's tribe, the Quraysh (pronounced koo-RAYSH), worshiped idols and had a lucrative trading business with people from all over Arabia who came to Mecca to worship at the Kaaba, their House of Idols. These pilgrims brought the Kaaba gifts, as well as many goods to trade with the people of Mecca. Because he was concerned that these people stop worshiping idols and also because of his interest in all the profit that the Meccans got through their trading, a Christian king of Yemen built a great cathedral and started to lure the idol-worshipers away from Mecca. Upset at the resulting loss of trade, some of the Quraysh people desecrated the cathedral by putting excrement on the walls, hoping to repulse people from entering. Enraged, the king of Yemen sent a battalion of soldiers to Mecca, with elephants borrowed from his friend, the king of Ethiopia, to destroy the House of Idols. Muhammad is said to have been born in "The Year of the Elephant," when this story took place.

Muhammad condemned idolatry (Noah 71:22-25) and wanted to destroy it. His desire was to teach his people to worship the one true God.

So some say it's not logical that later on, the Qur'an would say that God sent birds to defend these idol-worshipers by dropping stones on the elephants coming to Mecca to destroy the House of Idols (Elephant 105:1-5). A simple explanation to this is that God did not defend the idol-worshipers themselves but the Kaaba, which is supposed to have been built by His friend Abraham and Abraham's son. Perhaps the army accompanying the elephants got smallpox, which looks like stones on the skin, as some commentators have explained (see Pickthall's introduction to Elephant [Surah 105], page 732[1]).

Others object to the Qur'an because it calls Mary, the mother of Jesus ("Mariam" is the word for Mary in the Qur'an), "the daughter of Imran" (Forbidding 66:12; Imran was Moses' father) and also calls her the "sister of Aaron" (Mary 19:28; Aaron was Moses' brother). Yet these were biblical characters who lived over a thousand years before she was born. (Moses and Aaron did have a sister named Miriam.) The critics say Muhammad must have confused the Virgin Mary with Aaron's sister Miriam. Muslims explain the seeming contradiction by saying that Mary was the sister of Aaron and the daughter of Imran in terms of her sanctity, since both of them were holy women.

## Ishmael and Isaac

Most Muslims today say Abraham was asked to sacrifice Ishmael, not Isaac. But At-Tabbari, a famous Arab historian, fills several pages of his first volume with traditions (the traditions [hadith in Arabic] are of this form: "So-and-so heard from so-and-so, who heard from so-and-so, who heard from so-and-so . . . who heard from Muhammad) indicating that Ishmael was to be sacrificed and three more pages with traditions that say it was Isaac.[2] So, tradition gives equal support for both points of view. Here is the only passage in the Qur'an about the sacrifice, and it refers to Abraham's "son" without mentioning any name:

> [Abraham] said, "I am going to my Lord; He will guide me. My Lord, give me one of the righteous." Then We gave him the good tidings of a prudent boy; and when he had reached the age of running with him, he said, "My son, I see in a dream that I shall sacrifice thee; consider, what thinkest thou?"
>
> He said, "My father, do as thou art bidden; thou shalt find me, God willing, one of the steadfast."
>
> When they had surrendered, and he flung him upon his brow, We called unto him, "Abraham, thou hast confirmed the vision; even so We recompense the good-doers. This is indeed the manifest trial." And We ransomed him with a mighty sacrifice, and left for him among the later folk. "Peace be upon Abraham!" (Rangers 37:101-109)

Muhammad knew very well that the Qur'an could not contradict the Bible — or, if it did, he knew that such a profound kind
of difference would need to be made extremely clear. The Qur'an
says the Bible is the Word of God. The Qur'an itself confirms it.
Seven places in the Qur'an say the Word of God cannot be
changed and that no one can tamper with it. So again, there need
not be any contradiction in this case.

Please note that the most important point in the foregoing is
toward the end of the Qur'anic passage quoted here. It contains
all the gospel truth, the good news, in a nutshell. Let me explain.

The word "We" refers to God speaking here. He does not say
"I" in the singular. He speaks as the Sovereign, referring to Himself as "We" (in the plural). And, as in the case of any king who
speaks with a collective royal presence that implies his whole line
of royalty — past, present, and future — God is here including Himself as King, Word, and Spirit, forming the one and only God, who
cannot be divided into separate essences.

The words "ransomed" and "sacrifice" here emphasize the
sublime covenant nature that looked forward to the ultimate Sacrifice at the Cross. Why, in this passage from the Qur'an, did God
have to ransom the boy in order to set him free? Because anything
offered to God could not be taken back unless God replaced it with
something else, or redeemed it and paid for it. This was a sign of
God's perfect "sacrifice" to come, where God paid the ultimate
price with His own life (see Hebrews 11:17-19).

Arberry's translation of Rangers 37:107 refers to this as a
"mighty sacrifice." What could this "mighty" (other translations
refer to it as "momentous" and "valuable beyond estimation") sacrifice be? Some commentators on the Qur'an have said in essence,
"The Towrah [Old Testament] says a ram, but what kind of ram
could be 'valuable beyond estimation'? Even a billion rams have a
value that can be estimated." After deep reflection, they conclude
by saying, "God only knows." It is true that God knows, but
Muhammad also seems to have known. He had often discussed
with his Jewish and Christian friends the Christ, "the Lamb of God,

who takes away the sin of the world!" as John the Baptist (Yahya) called Him. Only about Christ can we truly say that here was a sacrifice "valuable beyond estimation" (see 1 Peter 1:18-19).

Abraham's son was loved by God because he was His friend's son. Any man or woman, any son or daughter, of Adam, God's representative (khalifah, Cow 2:30), is dearly beloved by Him. No matter who your Muslim friend may be, he or she is important to God. It's important for you to be able to discuss this story of Abraham and other stories familiar to Muslims if you plan to eventually bring Christ into true focus. As you do so, keep your wits about you. Be pure and innocent in your heart, in your motives, but be aware of what is respectful and what is offensive, what is appropriate and what is inappropriate and indiscreet. Your physical life and your friend's spiritual life may depend on it.

---

1. Mohammed Marmaduke Pickthall, *The Meaning of the Glorious Koran* (New York: The New American Library, Mentor Books, 1953).

2. This reference is from At-Tabbari's book, *Ta'rikh ar-rusul wa'l-muluk* (Annales, in French), ed. de Goeje (Leyde, 1879-1901), Volume 1, pp. 135-139.

# CHAPTER 8

# Guidelines for Sharing the Seven Muslim–Christian Principles

❦

I developed *The Seven Muslim-Christian Principles* (which has been published in booklet form) as an aid for people to use in befriending Muslims. More than 80 percent of Muslims who finish studying these seven principles come to put their trust in Christ—when the Christian who shares the principles does so in a way that is personally and culturally sensitive. Following the guidelines below as you work your way through the Seven Principles, which are covered in the following seven chapters, will help you create an environment that will enable your Muslim friend to be receptive to this process.

*The Seven Principles in this book are not like a tract to be passed out to your Muslim friend, but rather a study guide for you, which you can share in a tailored way with your friend.* Exposure to all the information from the Seven Principles at once could turn someone against the individual ideas contained in it.

For example, "Saleem" played sports with a Christian who was employed in the Middle East. The Christian let Saleem read the booklet *The Seven Principles* all at once, on his own, with no discussion between them. "It sounds like a Christian wrote this booklet to try to make Muslims into Christians," Saleem told his friend. He couldn't believe Jesus died on the cross, and his Western friend did not take the time to build up to that point slowly to help him see the logic and necessity of the Crucifixion, as well as the Qur'an's support of it. This Muslim then went to a Sunni Muslim authority to back up his anti-Christian beliefs. After that, he was unapproachable.

*These principles were not intended to be read in one or two sittings.* A possible exception to this would be a Muslim who is unusually ripe and prepared for the whole message of the gospel. But in the vast majority of cases, I suggest you go through one principle every week or two, according to your friend's ability to understand and accept the truth of the principles.

*Build a relationship of trust and friendship by getting together just to have fun and socialize.* Discussing spiritual things all the time could weigh too heavily on your friend. He must be reassured that you really care about him, and also that what you are sharing with him is acceptable to his culture and his religious background.

*The Seven Principles are not designed to be used for witnessing to all types of people.* Religious and political fanatics and closed-minded people in general will often just want to argue. They have their mind made up—period. It is stirring up a hornet's nest to try to discuss these principles with them. Be careful and discerning. These principles are for the pious, the open-minded, and the philosophical.

A secularized person who doesn't care what his culture's religious Book says may respond more positively to reading the Gospel of Matthew out loud together. In fact, this is a good approach for a wide range of people because they find the life of Jesus so attractive in Matthew. Christ is not religious in the way they expect. The concept of religion they are used to is formal: praying memorized prayers several times a day, always facing the same direction. Reading about the forgiving Christ who heals the helpless and rebukes the Pharisees' religious hypocrisy can be liberating.

Of the four Gospels, Matthew seems to be the most appropriate for Muslims. Mark refers to Jesus as the Son of God in the first verse of the first chapter—an immediate offense. John refers to the Son of God often. Luke was written by a non-Jew to a non-Semitic audience.

Matthew wrote for a Jewish audience. Arab Muslims and Jews are both Semites, and both claim to be descendants of Abraham. They also have close cultural similarities and a rural mentality. Jews of the first century and Muslims today both hold traditional family values within an agricultural society. Sheep are their main domestic animals, and they both slaughter sheep for their feasts. They even use many of the same postures in prayer: standing with hands raised, kneeling while sitting on one's feet, and prostrating oneself with head to the ground (to show submission of one's intellect to God). Jews and Muslims both look to Abraham as their spiritual father.

Even the genealogy in chapter 1 of Matthew interests Muslims. These are Christ's credentials. That genealogy is an easy way to point out that Christ is not a physical son of God. This prepares the way for an understanding of Jesus as God's Son because Jesus is from His essence, because He is His Word (John 1:1,14; Women 4:171). The Qur'an also adds "and a Spirit from Him" (Women 4:171).

*Be familiar with the Seven Principles as a whole.* Then, when a question comes up (for example, about Jesus being the Son of God), you can say, "We'll be studying that in detail later on, but let me give you a brief summary now." Thus you won't get bogged down in a particular doctrinal issue before your friend has even covered the basic groundwork necessary for him to understand the necessity of that specific belief.

*Be sensitive to your friend's reaction as you go through the Seven Principles.* Just because you start discussing them doesn't mean you have to finish them. If you see that your friend is not ready or open, keep his friendship and bide your time.

*Get your friend to read the verses with you from the Bible, and read with him from the Qur'an.* You can see his reaction as he reads. If it seems he doesn't understand something, stop and explain. Spend at least as much time discussing and explaining as you do in actual reading. If English is not his first language, go back over the difficult or technical words, rephrasing and explaining what they mean.

*Your main purpose is to expose your friend to the Word of God.* After all, "Faith comes from hearing the message, and the message is heard through the word of Christ" (Romans 10:17). Use the Qur'an because it is authoritative to your friend, just as Paul quoted the Greek poets (Acts 17:28) to make a point in convincing the people in Athens.

*If your friend has questions about Bible verses, look up the context.* Use a modern English translation of the Bible. Bring a Bible in his language to help explain the meaning of verses. You can get one from the American Bible Society (P.O. Box 5633, Grand Central Station, New York, NY 10163) or through a Christian bookstore. If your friend is Arabic-speaking, ask for *Today's Arabic Version* (which is the *Good News* translation) for the New Testament. If he speaks Farsi, ask for the *Good News* translation for the New Testament.

*Only take up one principle with your friend at a time.* Set aside at least one hour for each session.

*If your friend disagrees with the point of a principle, don't go on to the next one.* Wait. Pray. Deepen the friendship. Discuss. And then restudy the troublesome principle. The Seven Principles are sequential, and build on one another. Thus your Muslim friend must agree with the contents of the previous principle before you go on to the next one.

*If a verse in the Qur'an clearly makes the same point you are focusing on in one of the principles, emphasize that fact.* Since the principle is confirmed by his culture's religious book, it should be easy for him to accept.

*Give contextual background about Bible verses as much as possible.* Likewise, use other Bible passages that make the same point, since this will make the subject clearer. The object is to provide your friend with whatever background information will help him see how the individual points you are making fit in with the whole message of Scripture.

*The Seven Principles do not stress that only the Bible is the Word of God and that the Qur'an is not.* Why wave a red flag? At this point, your friend sees the Qur'an as above the Bible. Don't worry. Let the Bible stand on its own merit. Eventually it will all become clear, if only you let things sink in at a gradual pace. "'Let the prophet who has a dream tell his dream, but let the one who has my word speak it faithfully. For what has straw to do with grain?' declares the LORD. 'Is not my word like fire,' declares the LORD, 'and like a hammer that breaks a rock in pieces?'" (Jeremiah 23:28-29).

*It's ideal to share the Seven Principles with only one person alone, but it is fine in some situations to share the first few principles with two or three people at once.* Once again, exercise discretion.

*Be honest enough to acknowledge evil, even in your home country, and also the grave problems in the church.* Then your friend will see that what you're advocating is the truth of the Bible and not the wrong ways of Christians in the nominal, wayward church.

*Keep Satan bound and ineffective (Matthew 12:29) through prayer and fasting.* Remember that he will not relinquish anyone who is under his power without a fight. When you pray and fast, it can have a profound impact on you and on the effectiveness of your ministry. A group of Western and local Christians would meet on Thursdays in one Middle East country during the normal times for breakfast, lunch, and dinner to pray instead of eat for an hour. They would pray for all the nonChristian people they were witnessing to, and eventually saw good fruit from their dedication.

*You can monitor your contact's increasing growth toward belief by using a scale to measure his spiritual growth.* (See "The Engel Scale" in *How Can We Get Them to Listen* by Jim Engel.) One team of believers in the Middle East assigned each contact they were witnessing to a number according to where they were on their spiritual journey. Then they would know what to pray for and they would be able to see progress.

By keeping track of how your contact is progressing, you can be objectively encouraged about your Muslim friend's progress. Otherwise, sometimes the long hard wait seems *too* long, and the only recognizable progress that warrants any excitement is new birth, which takes a long time in coming. But if you use the Seven Principles with true sensitivity and creativity, you can expect to see life-changing results.

# CHAPTER 9

# PRINCIPLE ONE:
# God Has a Purpose
# for Our Lives

❦

I will explain the Seven Principles one by one, just as I would share them with a nonChristian, Muslim friend. Comments that I consider important to make to that friend along the way or points that need explanation to you will be inserted throughout the text. Remember that you should not use this book when you're right there with your friend. You can make your own notes and carry them with you, but bringing a book into the picture has the potential to complicate and confuse your personal communication unnecessarily.

Passages supporting each principle are taken from the Towrah (the Qur'an's word for the whole Old Testament), the Zabur (the Qur'an's word specifically for the Psalms), the Injeel (the Qur'an's word for the whole New Testament, not just the Gospels), and the Qur'an itself.

Although the Bible consists of sixty-six books with sixty-six titles, the Qur'an consists of one book with a different title for each of its 114 chapters ("Sura" in Arabic). To say Battlements 7:96 is the same as saying chapter (Sura) number 7 of the Qur'an, which is called "Battlements" (chapter 4 is called "Women," chapter 5 is called "Table," and so on). The numeral 96 indicates the verse number. When you look at the text of the Qur'an, you will notice that the verse number is placed at the end of the verse rather than the way it is done in the Bible, where the number is placed at the beginning of the verse.

I have included in each of the Seven Principles one verse from the Qur'an, along with three from the Bible, in order to explain the meaning of each principle more fully—what it says and what to do about it.

After winning the confidence of your friend, you could say, "There are seven important principles in the Bible that are supported by passages in the Qur'an. Would you be interested in studying them with me? I have an idea. Why don't you bring your Qur'an, and I'll bring my Bible, and we will study them together."

Then mention that scientists agree that certain discernible principles govern the behavior of everything in the universe. In a similar way, certain principles common to Judaism, Christianity, and Islam govern a person's relationship with God. By studying the books of these religions, we can understand these life-changing principles.

＊

The very first principle starts off as a positive step for you and your Muslim friend. It gets right to the point of our desire for ultimate meaning in life. Present this concept with a sense of genuine optimism, for there is real strength and hope in Principle 1: *God has a wonderful purpose for our lives.* The Creator of the universe loves us and wants to enrich us by having a close relationship with us. The following comments and passages from the Bible and the Qur'an should help you as you get your Muslim friend to catch the vision for the importance of this first principle.

◆ Ask your friend, "You and I together, as a Muslim and a Christian—what do we think is God's purpose in creating us? God is love. And He wants somebody to love, someone who is able to reciprocate this love.

Plants and animals cannot love Him. God wanted somebody who would respond to His love in a way that was meaningful to both Him and to that other being. So, God created man—in His image—and gave him everything he needed."

◆ Read out loud from the Qur'an (either your copy or your friend's copy) the story of the Fall in Cow 2:30-39 and Battlements 7:18-25. Then let him read out loud from the Bible the story of the Fall in Genesis 1:26-31, 3:1-24. If you find these readings too long, you may want to just select certain verses, or read them in several different sessions. After the reading, you may discuss the following points with your friend, or other similar things, according to what you think is needed to make him advance in his understanding of the things you want to tell him in the future.

◆ The Qur'an calls this man that God created His "khalifah," meaning representative. The Bible describes him as created "in the image of God" (Genesis 1:26-27). Ask your friend, "What do these things mean to you?" (Keep Genesis 1:26 in mind for a time later on when you discuss the oneness and plurality of God: "Let us make man in our image, in our likeness.")

◆ Discuss the different temptations used directly by Satan, as stated in the Qur'an, or by his agents, like the beautiful serpent, as in the Bible. Discuss how we are always tempted, how we fall, and the results of that fall.

◆ Discuss Genesis 3:15, without putting emphasis on Christ yet, but saying that God promised to send mankind a deliverer from Satan's power and his temptations. Note that this deliverer was to be from the seed of the woman only, and that there is no mention of the man having anything to do with His conception. Note also that in the Qur'an, He is called "God's guidance" at the end of the Fall story: "There shall come to you guidance from Me, and whosoever follows My guidance, no fear shall be on them, neither shall they sorrow" (Cow 2:38).

## Readings

### Towrah

Deuteronomy 7:9—Know therefore that the LORD your God is God; he is the faithful God, keeping his covenant of love to a thousand generations of those who love him and keep his commands.

### Zabur

Psalm 5:12—For surely, O LORD, you bless the righteous; you surround them with your favor as with a shield.

### Injeel

Luke 1:50—"His [God's] mercy extends to those who fear him, from generation to generation."

### Qur'an

Battlements 7:96—Had the people of the cities [around Mecca] believed and been godfearing, We [God] would have opened upon them blessings from heaven and earth.

All the above passages state in essence that God cares about the people He has created. Through the prophets and apostles, He has revealed His concern for us and His desire to give us inner peace, security, joy, purpose, strength, and guidance. All these come from a close relationship with God (a communion with Him and His wonderful attributes).

An ugly and lifeless electric light bulb is immediately changed as soon as you put it in contact (communion) with electrical power. It becomes full of life and brightness. It becomes beautiful, attractive, and beneficial to others, showing them the way to a life of usefulness and help to others. This is a picture of our lives *before* we know God and *after* we know Him and enter into full communion with Him. Here are some references to this kind of intimate communion with God from both the Bible and the Qur'an:

## Towrah

Isaiah 60:20 — "The LORD will be your everlasting light."

## Zabur

Psalm 16:11 — You have made known to me the path of life; you will fill me with joy in your presence, with eternal pleasures at your right hand.

Psalm 27:1 — The LORD is my light and my salvation — whom shall I fear? The LORD is the stronghold of my life — of whom shall I be afraid?

## Injeel

1 Peter 2:9 — You are a chosen people, a royal priesthood, a holy nation, a people belonging to God, that you may declare the praises of him who called you out of darkness into his wonderful light.

## Qur'an

Light 24:35 — God is the Light of the heavens and the earth; the likeness of His Light is as a niche wherein is a lamp (the lamp in a glass, the glass as it were a glittering star) kindled from a Blessed Tree, an olive that is neither of the East nor of the West whose oil wellnigh would shine, even if no fire touched it; Light upon Light; (God guides to His Light whom He will).

This beautiful description of God's light might have been inspired by the chandeliers that Muhammad saw in a large church during one of his trading trips to the Fertile Crescent countries. These lovely chandeliers were hung in the ceiling of the churches. They held lamps of glass full of pure olive oil from a blessed olive tree that belonged neither to the East nor to the West but to the whole world. On that oil floated lighted wicks that filled the church and the believers in it with their light. Similarly, God wants to attract whoever seeks Him to His light.

# CHAPTER 10
# PRINCIPLE TWO:
# Sin Separates Us from God

֍

The greatest of all our problems is that although God is our most primary need, we are faced with the seemingly impossible dilemma of Principle 2: *Sin separates us from the pleasure of God's company and all the resulting benefits.* This principle puts us in the position of admitting that there *is* such a thing as sin and that we all share in experiencing its devastating effects.

There are many aspects of this principle that will help you pursue a deep and meaningful discussion with your Muslim friend. But you must start with the most basic. The starting point is the "bad news." Even if we want to enjoy God's light, we have this problem that blocks us from that goal. The problem is sin. That's the bad news. There are many passages in both the Bible and the Qur'an that deal with this sin dilemma:

**Readings**

*Towrah*

Isaiah 59:2 — Your iniquities have separated you from your God; your sins have hidden his face from you, so that he will not hear.

## Zabur

Psalm 66:18—If I had cherished sin in my heart, the Lord would not have listened.

## Injeel

1 John 1:10—If we claim we have not sinned, we make him [God] out to be a liar and his word has no place in our lives.

## Qur'an

Cow 2:81—"Whoso earns evil, and is encompassed by his transgression—those are the inhabitants of the Fire; there they shall dwell forever."

This verse from the Qur'an has the same meaning as "The wages of sin is death" (Romans 6:23). By sinning, we earn or get paid our just "wages" of evil consequences. Cow 2:81 says a sinner is surrounded and overcome by his sin. So he goes to hell forever. Man was created to enjoy a continuous, close relationship with God. But he stubbornly abandoned Him to go his own, independent way. The Bible calls such rebellion or passive indifference toward God by several names, including sin, disobedience, and breaking God's law.

*

What's the difference between active rebellion and passive indifference toward God? Why, do you think, passive indifference is also counted as sin? Which in your opinion is more common: active rebellion or passive indifference toward God? These are good questions to grapple with. But the vitally important step here is to help your friend recognize and acknowledge that there *is* such a thing as sin.

Sin is not only bad news—it's the worst possible news. Why? Because it separates us from God. As a result of that separation, we have feelings of fear, frustration, emptiness, guilt, lack of purpose, lack of peace, and unhappiness. If we actively pursue sin, it shows that we are addicted, that we are pursuing self-destructive behavior, which is a symptom of disease. But even if we passively ignore God, we set ourselves up as gods, as the ultimate judges of what is right and wrong.

Most people tend to be evasive about sin. They might prefer to think of their sins more as errors or mistakes. Many people do not believe that mankind is sinful at all, but view our species as basically good. If that is the perspective of your Muslim friend, the more you drive home your point by telling the truth from different angles with this variety of verses, the more the logic of the truth will sink in.

If your companion is already convinced of the wages of sin, you do not need to spend much time on these remaining verses about sin. Just share as much as you think is necessary. Do not go more quickly than your friend can understand it. He has to assimilate all this.

## Readings

### Towrah

1 Kings 8:46—"There is no one who does not sin."

Ezekiel 18:20—"The soul who sins is the one who will die."

Hosea 8:7—"They sow the wind and reap the whirlwind."

## Zabur

Psalm 51:5—Surely I was sinful at birth, sinful from the time my mother conceived me.

Psalm 130:3—If you, O LORD, kept a record of sins, O Lord, who could stand?

Psalm 143:2—Do not bring your servant into judgment, for no one living is righteous before you [God].

## Injeel

Romans 3:10—"There is no one righteous, not even one."

Romans 3:23—All have sinned and fall short of the glory of God.

Galatians 6:7—Do not be deceived: God cannot be mocked. A man reaps what he sows.

1 John 1:8—If we claim to be without sin, we deceive ourselves and the truth is not in us.

## Qur'an

Winds 51:59-60—The evildoers shall have their portion, like the portion of their fellows; so let them not hasten Me [God]! So woe to the unbelievers, for that day [from that day] of theirs that they are promised.

Spider 29:40—Each We [God] seized [caught] for his sin; and of them against some We loosed a squall of pebbles [pits inside of dates] and some were seized by the Cry [plague], and some We made the earth to swallow, and some We drowned; God would never wrong them, but they wronged themselves.

✳

These two passages from the Qur'an have much to say about the progression from sin to judgment. Winds 51:59-60 indicates that those who *are* evil and *do* evil will get their punishment. Don't rush God to punish them, because it will be a terrible day for them when God starts giving them their punishment. In Spider 29:40 we see that God catches each person for all the sins that person has committed. Some of the people referred to in this verse were stoned and others were seized by a plague. Some were swallowed up by the earth, and some were drowned. The point here is that God deals with sin. Emphasize to your friend that each person is dealt with for his sin, and that God does not wrong them when He punishes them, but they wrong themselves by sinning, which inevitably bears the fruit of the punishment.

Some people say there is no sense of sin in the Qur'an. But these Qur'anic verses clearly show differently. They stress the consequences of sin. Since it is a common belief that man is not sinful, here are some extra verses from the Qur'an to hopefully help your friend see the truth on this point:

## Readings

### Qur'an

Rome 30:10 — The end of those that did evil was evil.

Cow 2:30 — When thy Lord said to the angels, "I am setting in the earth a viceroy." They said, "What, wilt Thou set therein one who will do corruption there, and shed blood?"

Here God is telling the angels before the Eden creation that He is going to put someone on earth to represent Him, namely man. "What?" the angels say. "But man will ruin the earth with his sin."

> Cow 2:36—Then Satan caused them [Adam and Eve] to slip therefrom [from the Garden of Eden] and brought them out of that they were in.

> Battlements 7:22-23—Their Lord [the Lord of Adam and Eve] called to them, "Did not I prohibit you from this tree, and say to you, 'Verily Satan is for you a manifest foe'?" They said, "Lord, we have wronged ourselves, and if Thou dost not forgive us, and have mercy upon us, we shall surely be among the lost."

There is nothing in these preceding passages about good deeds saving us from our sin. They say that we are sinners and that if God does not forgive and save us, we are lost. Teachers of Muslim theology do not typically mention original sin, but here it is in the Qur'an. Some say the Christian church invented sin in order to have Christ as a Savior. But Muhammad serves as a witness against this interpretation.

> Ta Ha 20:121—Adam disobeyed his Lord, and so he erred.

> Abraham 14:34—Surely man is sinful, unthankful!

> Confederates 33:72—Surely he [man] is sinful, very foolish.

These three verses all reiterate Romans 3:23. Emphasize the last two, for they are so clear. Drive home the point that these verses are from the Muslim's book of authority.

> House of Imran 3:11—God seized them because of their sins; God is terrible in retribution.

Creator 35:10—Those who devise evil deeds—theirs shall
be a terrible chastisement, and their devising shall come to
naught.

Bee 16:34—So the evil things that they wrought [made]
smote them, and they were encompassed by that they
mocked at.

These three preceding passages show that people's sin just
boomerangs. The one who makes a trap for someone else falls into
it. Your sins will find you out. Make light of sin, and that same sin
will get *you*.

Crouching 45:7-8—"Woe to every guilty impostor who
hears the signs [miracles, or message] of God being recited
to him, then perseveres in waxing proud [goes on sinning],
as if he has not heard them."

Cow 2:276—God loves not any guilty ingrate.

If you discuss these passages with your friend and believe
that he has been willing to acknowledge that sin is a reality—a
reality that affects all of us—then you could probably speak
directly and personally to him about the sin reality. To a Muslim,
communicating the dimension of sin that we would call *defilement*
is very important. Muslims are constantly aware of the importance
of being "clean." But as Jesus pointed out, although being clean
on the outside is important, being clean on the *inside* is far more
important (Matthew 23:25-28). Until a person sees that he is dirty
on the inside, then he has no real sense of sin, and thus no perceived need for being saved.

Ask your friend outright, "Are you willing to admit that you
have sinned?" Don't be so immediate in your wording as to say,
"Are you willing to admit that you are sinning?"

Your own admission ("I know *I* have!") makes it less threatening for him to admit the same thing. Then if he admits his sin-fulness, ask, "What do you think you can do to remove it?" This may leave him temporarily hanging, but it leads logically to the third principle, which gets to the heart of how bad the bad news of sin really is. Set up an appointment to discuss that next vital truth with your friend.

# CHAPTER 11
# PRINCIPLE THREE:
# We Can't Save Ourselves

⚭

When it comes to what we can actually *do* about our sin problem, we find that human efforts won't work. We must ultimately look to God for *His* solution. Thus we arrive at Principle 3: *We are helpless to save ourselves from this dilemma of sin and death.* Let's take a look at the specifics of how you can dialogue with your Muslim friend about this principle.

First, it is vitally important that your companion see that he cannot save himself from his sin by his good works, just as you cannot get sweet water from a bitter spring. Many people believe that good deeds or "a good life" can save us. But there are many passages in both the Bible and the Qur'an that contradict this concept of salvation through good works:

## Readings

### *Towrah*

> Proverbs 14:12 — There is a way that seems right to a man, but in the end it leads to death.

## Zabur

Psalm 125:5 — Those who turn to crooked ways the LORD will banish with the evildoers.

## Injeel

Titus 3:4-5 — God our Savior . . . saved us, not because of righteous things we had done, but because of his mercy. He saved us through the washing of rebirth and renewal by the Holy Spirit.

## Qur'an

Cattle 6:70 — Remind hereby, lest a soul should be given up to destruction for what it [the soul] has earned [deserved]; apart from God, it [the soul] has no protector and no intercessor; though it offer any equivalent, it shall not be taken from it [the soul].

What Cattle 6:70 is saying, in other words, is, "Beware lest you receive the destruction your sinful soul deserves because of what you have done. Outside of God, you have no hope of being saved — no protector and no one to intercede for you. Though your soul tries to offer something 'big,' nothing is equivalent to what is necessary to save you. Nothing can save you but God."

*

Man plans to remove his own sin by being good. He tries to out-weigh his bad deeds with good deeds, such as religious works, actions benefiting mankind, and political activity. But man forgets that the only righteousness he can produce comes out of an unclean life, since he is a sinner. So, self-produced righteousness is also unclean. As the Towrah says in Isaiah 64:6, "All of us have become like one who is unclean, and all our righteous acts are like filthy rags."

Wearied and miserable due to sinful living, a man decided to take the long walk to ask advice of a godly friend. When he arrived, he immediately explained that guilt, frustration, and fear were tormenting him day and night. He asked his friend, "What works can I do to relieve these feelings, and find peace of mind and happiness?"

Before answering, the friend ordered his servant to bring a cold drink for this exhausted visitor. The servant soon returned with the drink. But before offering it to his friend, the host added a large drop of ink, blackening the drink. The guest asked, "What are you doing?"

"Just answering your question," he replied. "You won't accept this drink because I spoiled it with a drop of ink. Yet you want a pure and holy God to accept your good deeds when you have defiled them with the filthy sins of your heart and mind!"

The man understood the lesson. Right then and there he asked God for His pardon and cleansing. Understanding the bad news of sin led him to seek out the good news of God that effectively deals with that sin.

As you talk with your friend, emphasize that bad deeds *always* outweigh good deeds—because a sinner's good deeds are unacceptable. And so, because man is thus unable to please God, he must trust in Him and in what He says. It's a matter of a major step of humility and commitment before God. Take a look at what the Bible and the Qur'an have to say about this solution to sin:

## Readings

### Towrah

> Genesis 15:6—Abram [Abraham] believed the LORD, and he [God] credited it to him as righteousness.

2 Chronicles 20:20—"Have faith in the LORD your God and you will be upheld; have faith in his prophets and you will be successful."

Habakkuk 2:4—"The righteous [person] will live by his faith."

## Zabur

Psalm 13:5—I trust in your unfailing [steadfast] love; my heart rejoices in your salvation.

Psalm 32:1—Blessed is he whose transgressions are forgiven, whose sins are covered.

Psalm 85:7-9—Show us your unfailing love, O LORD, and grant us your salvation. . . . Surely [God's] salvation is near [at hand for] those who fear him.

## Injeel

Romans 14:23—Everything that does not come from faith is sin.

Ephesians 2:8-9—It is by grace you have been saved, through faith—and this not from yourselves, it is the gift of God—not by works, so that no one can boast.

Hebrews 11:6—Without faith it is impossible to please God, because anyone who comes to him must believe that he exists and that he rewards those who earnestly seek him.

## Qur'an

> Believers 23:109 (Dawood)—"Among My servants there
> were those who said: 'Lord, we believe in You. Forgive us
> and have mercy on us: You are the best of those that show
> mercy [the most merciful One].'"

Believers 23:109 says in essence that there are people who understand they must throw themselves on the mercy of God because their own deeds are not enough. This is why the Qur'an also says, "Your Lord has prescribed for Himself mercy. Whosoever of you does evil in ignorance, and thereafter repents and makes amends, He is All-forgiving, All-compassionate" (Cattle 6:54).

Emphasize to your friend that believing and asking God for mercy brings forgiveness, according to the following verse:

> Muhammad 47:19—Ask forgiveness for thy
> [Muhammad's] sin, and for the believers, men and
> women. God knows your going to and fro, and your
> lodging.

It is clear from this verse from the Qur'an that no one can escape the need for forgiveness. Even Muhammad had the sin problem.

> Cow 2:256-257—No compulsion is there in religion. . . .
> Whoever disbelieves in idols and believes in God, has laid
> hold of the most firm handle, unbreaking; God is All-
> hearing, All-knowing. God is the Protector of the believers;
> He brings them forth from the shadows into the light.

In other words, you cannot force people to accept a religion they do not like. They have to choose on their own to leave idols and believe in God, to lay hold of Him with a sense of commitment— "the most firm handle." God Himself is your protector, *not* your good deeds. God alone is your Savior. He takes people out of darkness ("the shadows") into His wonderful light.

> House of Imran 3:193 — "Our Lord, we have heard a caller
> [a person calling others to hear, believe, and repent],
> calling us to belief, saying, 'Believe you in your Lord!' And
> we believe. Our Lord, forgive Thou us our sins and acquit
> us of our evil deeds, and take us to Thee with the pious
> [the righteous]."

This verse is plain. In effect it says, "Believe and receive forgiveness for past and present sins." Ask your friend a question that will focus in on the heart of this issue: "How many times have you tried unsuccessfully to change your sinful life, or to conquer a bad habit?" Remind your friend that we are all sinners — you and everyone else. Also, reassure him that countless other sinful people have succeeded — through God's help. Specifically ask your friend if he wants to be one of them.

How is this accomplished? This leads logically to the next step. Set up an appointment to go over Principle 4. Keep everything upbeat. Be sure to spend social time and fun time together.

# CHAPTER 12
# PRINCIPLE FOUR:
# The Cross Is the Bridge to Life

ॐ

Though we find ourselves in the seemingly impossible situation of being doomed in a cesspool of sin and death, there is still hope. This is where we come to see the vital importance of Principle 4: *God has provided a solution to our dilemma.* Help your Muslim friend see that the emphasis here is on *God.* Our only hope when we're in an impossible situation is to turn to the only One who can do the impossible.

＊

One of the reasons why God created the universe was that He wanted to commune with creatures who were like Himself, who bear His very image. God cared so much about us that even after Adam and Eve ushered us into the darkness of sin, He worked out His own plan to save us since we couldn't save ourselves. There are many passages in both the Bible and the Qur'an that emphasize the fact that God did for us what we couldn't do for ourselves: He solved our sin problem — but at great cost to Himself.

## Readings

### Towrah

> Isaiah 19:20—When they cry out to the LORD because of
> their oppressors, he will send them a savior and defender,
> and he will rescue [deliver] them.

### Zabur

> Psalm 49:7-8—No man can redeem the life of another or
> give to God a ransom for him—the ransom for a life is
> costly, no payment is ever enough.

Isn't it interesting that it is impossible for a person to do enough to
ransom oneself from the just punishment for his sins? It's too big
a job. (See also Romans 3:20.)

### Injeel

> Ephesians 2:8-9—It is by grace you have been saved,
> through faith—and this not from yourselves, it is the gift of
> God—not by works, so that no one can boast.

### Qur'an

> Rangers 37:107—We [God] ransomed him [Abraham's
> son] with a mighty sacrifice.

The term "mighty" in Arabic also means priceless without any
limit. No one is like that but Christ. Sharing this concept with your
friend will raise his curiosity and revive the eternal feelings within
him. Since God is the only one able to provide for man's ransom,
man must look to God in order to be saved.

＊

The Eastern mind loves stories. The following story will enable your hearer to see how God has taken the punishment for man's sin Himself.

A man was brought to court for stealing money from his company. As the judge asked him the usual questions, he discovered that this man had been his childhood friend. That put the judge in a predicament. The tender spot in his heart for his friend made him want to not condemn the man to the imprisonment he deserved. But to free him would be unfair to his employer, who had been wronged.

After much thought, the judge himself repaid the company all the money the man had stolen. The representatives of the company were satisfied. The man himself was freed, and was grateful to the judge for the rest of his life.

In the same way, although we stand rightly condemned for our sins, God, in His love for us, took our punishment by giving Himself as a mighty sacrifice for us at the cross. This story might plant some good seeds in your friend's mind about the logic of God being both righteous and merciful, both "just and the one who justifies those who have faith in Christ" (Romans 3:26). This story might also give some perspective to your friend's thinking about the doctrine of the Trinity.

＊

It is vitally important to recognize the significance of the Cross. The underlying concept is one of paying a ransom for another person. A ransom is the necessary price to pay for the release of a captive. Your friend must see that *he* is a captive—that all of us are captives to sin. Then the Cross will begin to be far more logical, necessary, and appealing as a concept. The following verses from the Bible and the Qur'an further document that God should be trusted to provide man's ransom from his sin.

## Readings

### *Towrah*

> Genesis 22:13 — Abraham looked up and there in a thicket he saw a ram caught by its horns. He went over and took the ram and sacrificed it as a burnt offering instead of his son.

> Exodus 12:13 — "The blood will be a sign for you on the houses where you are; and when I see the blood, I will pass over you. No destructive plague will touch you when I strike Egypt."

Notice that just as God designated that the blood of a pure lamb (without defect) would be a sign to protect the Jews in Egypt from being destroyed by a plague of death, so trusting in the pure blood of God's mighty sacrifice at the cross protects us from being destroyed in hell because of our sins.

> Leviticus 17:11 — "It is the blood that makes atonement for one's life."

Pure blood is necessary for our sins to be sufficiently paid for in God's sight — life for life. Pure blood covered the sin of Adam and Eve when God killed an animal and used its skin to cover their nakedness (see Genesis 3:21).

> Isaiah 63:8 — [God] said, "Surely they are my people, sons who will not be false to me;" and so he became their Savior.

The point here is that God Himself is the Savior of His people.

## Zabur

> Psalm 34:22 — The LORD redeems his servants; no one will be condemned who takes refuge in him.

> Psalm 31:5 — Into your hands I commit my spirit; redeem me, O LORD, the God of truth.

> Psalm 56:13 — You have delivered me from death and my feet from stumbling, that I may walk before God in the light of life.

We see in Psalm 34:22 that taking refuge in God will save you from condemnation. In other words, God alone can redeem and deliver us, which we see clearly in Psalms 31:5 and 56:13. We can't redeem ourselves by trying to make our good deeds outweigh our bad ones. Since God Himself is singled out as the One who redeems and delivers, obviously He recognizes that we need that for our lives — being delivered from the power of sin, from having to continue sinning.

> Psalm 107:6-7 — Then they cried out to the LORD in their trouble, and he delivered them from their distress. He led them by a straight way.

Many Muslims ask God to lead them in a straight path at least five times a day. Psalm 107:6-7 shows that the Bible agrees with this prayer, and that indeed we have to look to God alone for our salvation and not trust in ourselves.

## Injeel

> Matthew 26:28 — "This is my blood [Jesus' blood] of the covenant, which is poured out for many for the forgiveness of sins."

Romans 3:23-25 — All have sinned and fall short of the glory of God, and are justified freely by his grace through the redemption that came by Christ Jesus. God presented him as a sacrifice of atonement through faith in his blood. He did this to demonstrate his justice, because in his forbearance he had left the sins committed beforehand unpunished.

In Matthew 26:28, Jesus Himself explains that pure blood is necessary for forgiveness. (That concept is fully explained in Hebrews 9.) Romans 3:23-25 goes on to emphasize that we are all fallen sinners who need the redemption that is available in Jesus, not in our own efforts. The necessity of pure blood is mentioned again. This shows how amazing God's plan for us really is, for because of His mighty sacrifice of Himself through Christ, He cancels out our past sins so that we do not have to pay for them. Why? Because Jesus had already done so. (See also 1 Peter 1:18-19.)

## Qur'an

Story 28:16 — He [Moses] said, "My Lord, I have wronged myself. Forgive me!" So God forgave him, for He is the All-forgiving, the All-compassionate.

Some people say that prophets (like Moses) do not sin. But this verse shows that even a prophet needs to be rescued from sin.

If your friend does not agree with you, do not worry. You have put the thought in his mind. Some people are like burned buildings. The frame of truth is still there, but so much of it has been destroyed. You have to build it back up stone by stone by planting these seed thoughts of truth in his mind.

Cow 2:38 — "There shall come to you [Adam and Eve] guidance from Me [God], and whosoever follows My guidance, no fear shall be on them, neither shall they sorrow."

There was guidance even for Adam and Eve when they sinned—if they looked to the Lord for it. That is, the Lord Himself was their salvation. They couldn't depend on their own works.

> Women 4:110—Whosoever does evil, or wrongs himself, and then prays God's forgiveness, he shall find God is All-forgiving, All-compassionate.

People often believe that their good deeds must outweigh their bad deeds to win God's favor and to go to heaven. This verse says they must repent and ask for God's forgiveness of their bad deeds. Sharing this verse will help sow in your friend's heart a brand-new thought.

Here's a story that can bring this point home. To get rid of her anger every time her son hurt her, a widow pounded a nail in the back of her kitchen door. One day the son opened the door and saw all the nails. "What is the meaning of these?" he asked her. Reluctantly, she told him. Amazed that he had hurt her so much, he asked her to forgive him. And he removed all the nails.

But the holes remained, reminding him that he had hurt her so much. The nail prints served as a sign to keep him from hurting her again.

We have to come to God ourselves for forgiveness, according to Cattle 6:69. Even when He forgives us, we still have the memory of what we have done to be a deterrent to repeating the same sins.

These verses may begin to seem repetitive after a while. But the more of this basic concept you share from both the Bible and the Qur'an, the more the point is driven home. The purpose in using the Qur'an so much in witnessing is to let your Muslim friend see how much Muhammad revered the Bible. Your friend will find that the verses you show him in the Qur'an and the Bible are saying the same thing. This will gradually open his heart to the truth.

✳

Jane, a Christian, went to a Middle Eastern country to study Arabic in the late 1970s. She and her Middle Eastern girlfriend rented a portion of a house belonging to a Muslim widow and her ten children. They could not speak any English, and Jane could only speak a few words of Arabic. But the family welcomed the two women. The sons would fix anything of theirs that broke. And Jane would go across the hallway to their bungalow to practice her Arabic.

Her roommate warned her that her actions in Arab culture might be perceived by the family as an attempt to get one of their sons for a husband. So, she disciplined herself to keep her gaze downward around the men, and to avoid laughing and talking with them. But while the sons were at school and work, Jane would visit the women at home for longer and longer periods of time.

She grew to love the family deeply and became heavily burdened to share Christ with them, but she could not communicate in Arabic, so she looked for a way to build a relationship. The children were basically ignored in the family, so Jane, who loved children, would take the children swimming and on picnics. The oldest son regularly disappeared on his day off and didn't spend any time with his younger siblings, as he would normally be expected to do. Jane also baked birthday cakes for all the members of the family. This was a special treat since birthdays are not celebrated in Arab culture.

One day, the widow had to go to the hospital to have her arthritic knee operated on. Nurses in that country would only take her temperature and check her blood pressure. Middle Easterners generally look down on nursing as menial work. Jane, a nurse, went to the hospital all day for the two days following the widow's surgery to give the woman postoperative care. She would get her to cough, make sure her leg was elevated, give her back rubs, and make sure she was clean. It took two people to turn her in bed. All this made a deep impression on the widow.

Later, the oldest daughter and her husband were planning to go to Chicago to look into the possibility of moving there. Before they left, Jane casually said, "Oh, I wish you could visit my parents in Minneapolis." To Jane's astonishment, they did.

The next year, the daughter and her husband returned. Thanksgiving and the Feast of Sacrifice (a big Muslim holiday to celebrate Abraham being willing to sacrifice his son to God) were close together that year. So Jane invited the widow's family for an American-style Thanksgiving dinner, and also to celebrate the big feast at the same time.

Their country practically closes down for a week to celebrate this feast. There is a holiday spirit in the air. Everyone goes home to be with parents and family. They slaughter sheep in memory of the sheep Abraham offered to God instead of his son. Thus, all twenty-two members of the widow's extended family were home. They all wanted to attend Jane's dinner, especially the oldest daughter, who wanted her family to see what an American Thanksgiving was like.

The Qur'an explains that when God halted Abraham from killing his son, He provided him a sheep, saying, "And We [God] ransomed him [Abraham's son] with a mighty sacrifice [in other words, valuable beyond estimation]" (Rangers 37:107). This can be used as an analogy to explain how Jesus, the perfect Lamb of God, was that mighty sacrifice, valuable beyond estimation, sacrificing Himself on our behalf to bring us to God.

Jane wanted to capitalize on the Feast of Sacrifice to explain the gospel to the Muslim family, but she could not do it in Arabic. So she prayed, "Who can I invite to share the meaning of the feast with them?" She thought of an Arab Christian in town who could share sensitively without preaching at them, but he would be on a trip at that time.

"Lord, who would be the best person to do this?" she prayed. Then she thought of me. I would often use this story in the Qur'an to explain the Cross. But I lived in a different country and the dinner was only a week away. She thought it was ridiculous, but she sent me a telegram, inviting me anyway.

I had been trying unsuccessfully to get a visa to visit for those dates. This was strange, for I had never had trouble before. On receiving Jane's telegram, I knew this was why I had not been able to get a visa to that country. I responded to Jane by telegram, saying that I would come. All the travel agencies were closed for the holidays, but with much prayer, God enabled me to get a ticket and fly there.

I had Jane's language teacher's phone number and address, and I knew what area Jane lived in, but I did not know exactly where, so I asked a taxi to take me to the language teacher's house. It was off the main street. A person had to follow back roads to get there. The taxi driver turned off the main street to the left and turned down the twisting streets toward Jane's area. Stopping in front of Jane's house, the taxi driver asked one of the widow's children, "Where does the American lady live?" The child pointed to his house.

Jane was not at home. Because she didn't have a stove, she was at an Arab Christian's home—baking pumpkin pies. But when her Muslim family realized that I was her guest, Arab hospitality took over. The men, dressed as they were in their pajamas and drinking coffee, welcomed me.

They knew I was a Christian by my name, but when I would say, "The Qur'an says . . . ," they were amazed that a Christian would know the Qur'an so well.

Jane arrived home two hours later, giving me lots of time to get to know them. The children ran to tell her the news, "Miss Jane, Miss Jane . . ."

She had been worried about how she would explain to them who I was and why I came, if I did (she never received my telegram). Seeing what had happened, she said, "I could not have introduced him better. Arabs respect old people. And they respected him. He was loving and gracious and had them eating out of his hand." She told them I was an old friend of hers who had come to share the Feast with them the next day. They never asked her why.

Jane was exhausted from cooking for days. Everyone sat in a circle on the floor as Arabs do, placing the food in the center of them on a tablecloth. They were all eager to taste the unusual American dishes. I told Jane in English, "When you serve the dessert, I will start." Not knowing what would happen, she was nervous and excited.

I asked them what was the true meaning of the Feast. Lots of dialogue began between the men, who were nominal Muslims. The women, who were the religious ones, were silent and eventually left to take care of the noisy children. The family members hardly knew the story of Abraham sacrificing his son. So I went over the whole story. "Who is this being sacrificed?" I asked them.

"Ishmael," they answered.

"Does the Qur'an say that?" I asked. They looked and saw that it only said "his son" without naming him. "When there is any question as to what the Qur'an means, Sura 10:94 [Jonah] says that we should go back to the Bible to find the answer," I told them, and read the verse to them: "If thou art in doubt regarding what We [God] have sent down [the Qur'an] to thee, ask those who recite the Book before thee. The truth has come to thee from thy Lord." They could then see that Genesis 22 clearly stated that it was Isaac.

I then told them that although the name may seem unimportant to some people, At-Tabbari filled nearly three pages of his famous history book At-tabaqat (pages 135-137) with traditions that say the boy was Ishmael. Then he filled the next three pages (pages 137-139) with traditions that say he was Isaac.[1]

The atmosphere was congenial. The men were hanging on every word. They were not threatened that their Muslim beliefs were being challenged, and they did not argue or raise their voices, as is common when a Christian witnesses to a Muslim whom he has not first inundated with love and respect.

"What is this mighty sacrifice?" I asked them. It was obvious, from the Arabic word for mighty ('azim), that the big sheep (or ram) that Abraham found in the bushes was not the mighty sacrifice.

"Maybe it was one thousand camels," someone said.

"What would be the greatest thing that God could sacrifice?" I asked them. After some discussion, I said, "The biggest sacrifice that God could give would be Himself, as we read in Cattle 6:12: 'He [God] has prescribed for Himself mercy.' This is why He came to the world in the person of Christ, as we are told in Women 4:171, 'The Messiah, Jesus son of Mary, was . . . the Messenger of God, and His Word that He committed to Mary, and a Spirit from Him.' God's Word and Spirit," I added, "were with Him before all time, and can never be separated from Him. Otherwise He would be mute, without Word, or dead, without spirit."

I pointed out that God had, on several past occasions, shown Himself to people in different ways. For instance, God revealed Himself in a burning bush to Moses, as it is stated in Ant 27:7-9: "When Moses said to his people 'I observe a fire, and will bring you news of it, or I will bring you a flaming brand, that haply you shall warm yourselves.' So, when he came to it, he was called: 'Blessed is He who is in the fire, and he who is about it. Glory be to God, the Lord of all Being! Moses, behold, it is I, God, the All-mighty, the All-wise.'" I mentioned then that it is not such a strange thing that a God with this kind of incredible power and creativity would choose conception and birth through a pure virgin woman to enter Himself into the world. All this finally led into a lengthy discussion of Christ's death—as the perfect Lamb of God being sacrificed for our salvation.

For two hours we talked. They were really thinking deeply about all these new things they were hearing about for the first time. Before closing the time we had together, I challenged them to read and study the Bible. But none of them owned one. Jane had an Arabic one that she let me give to the son, who was a university professor. He received it with considerable joy and interest.

Previously, Jane's roommate had befriended a sixteen-year-old girl on the street who had leukemia—cancer of the blood. They went to see a Moody science film about blood, and this resulted in the girl's conversion. She talked to everyone about Christ up until her death.

Sometime after the Thanksgiving dinner, Jane's Arabic had improved enough that she was able to tell the widow how Christ changed her life, just as He had changed the sixteen-year-old girl's life. But six months after the feast, Jane left the country. It was heart-wrenching for her to leave her Muslim family. The widow and Jane both wept as they said goodbye.

The Feast was that family's first exposure to the gospel. The relationship God gave Jane with that family and the miracles He performed to get me there lead me to believe that the seed sown will somehow germinate as part of God's eternal plan in the Muslim world. This experience serves as an example of one way to communicate the fourth principle, namely, that God has provided the solution to the sin problem.

---

1. The reference here is to At-Tabbari's book, *Ta'rikh ar-rusul wa'l-muluk* (Annales, in French), ed. de Goeje (Leyde, 1879-1901), Volume 1, pp. 135-139.

# CHAPTER 13
# PRINCIPLE FIVE:
# God's Provision Is a Person

⟨❦⟩

W hen you reach this point in the Seven Principles, you are close to giving your friend a full perspective of spiritual truth. But you may find a unique kind of resistance when you speak of truth being embodied in a person, especially since the person most highly revered in the Muslim world is Muhammad. So, you can see the pivotal nature of Principle 5: *The solution is not just the Cross but a divine Person, Jesus Christ, who was anointed by the Holy Spirit and called the Word of God.*

Exactly who was—and is—Jesus Christ? This is a question you need to answer in a thorough way, but with respect, being constantly aware of what is commonly taught within Muslim culture. That's why it's especially important in Principle 5 to refer to passages from both the Bible and the Qur'an in order to give credibility to what you are saying.

Both the Qur'an and the Bible say Christ is the Word of God, who is anointed and aided by the Holy Spirit. So it is legitimate to use these terms and to avoid certain other terms that will raise unnecessary discussions and strife due to misunderstandings your friend has encountered in the past. When you stick with terms that are not emotionally loaded, your hearers will be more apt to listen to your perspective on Christ. In general, even those who do not trust Christ will reject Him not because of theological reasons but because of family or cultural pressures.

Be sure to say to your friend at this point, "It's interesting—and very logical—that God's provision is not a philosophical or a religious idea, not a list of rules to follow or a way of life. It's a person." In Principle 5, you are essentially giving this concept to the person you're talking to, and then you drive the point home with all the following verses.

## Readings

### Towrah

> Isaiah 61:1—The Spirit of the Sovereign LORD is on me, because the LORD has anointed me to preach good news to the poor . . . to proclaim freedom for the captives.

Here the prophet Isaiah talks about the coming Christ, or Messiah. When speaking with Arab Muslims, use the term "Christ" and not "Jesus" (Yasu) to avoid an argument, because they call Jesus Isa. Arab Christians and Muslims both call Jesus the Messiah. Using this shared name when speaking to them prevents added difficulties.

### Zabur

> Psalm 107:20—He sent forth his word and healed them; he rescued them from the grave.

God sent Christ—the Word—to the world to heal us from sin and so deliver us from sin's destruction.

## Injeel

> John 1:1,14—In the beginning was the Word, and the
> Word was with God, and the Word was God. . . . The Word
> became flesh and made his dwelling among us. We have
> seen his glory, the glory of the One and Only . . . full of
> grace and truth.

God's Word was with Him for all eternity. After all, He was always
able to speak. He sent this Word to us as a flesh-and-blood person
to save us from our sins.

## Qur'an

> House of Imran 3:45—When the angels said, "Mary, God
> gives thee good tidings of a Word from Him whose name is
> Messiah, Jesus, son of Mary; high honoured shall he be in
> this world and the next, near stationed to God."

✳

Point out to your friend that Christ is the Word of God, that He
was highly honored when He was in this world and that now He
is in the closest possible position with God, or, as the Injeel puts it,
"at the right hand of God" (Hebrews 10:12).

Then tell the story of Gabriel coming to the Virgin Mary to
tell her she would bear God's Word, Christ. Ask your friend, "What
other prophet has ever been born of a virgin?" This speaks of the
holiness of Christ, God's Word. It was foretold by God in the
Towrah (Genesis 3:15) immediately after Adam and Eve's disobedience. God said the seed of the woman—not the seed of the
man—shall crush Satan's head.

Explain also to your friend that even when a word is uttered
by God, it has not been severed from God. In this case we are talking about *the* Word of God. There is something extremely unique
about Christ. As a "word," He is an embodiment of what God

wants to communicate to us. As an eternal person, He is now right next to God, never apart from God, and thus a part *of* God.

A man once asked his friend, "Which came first: God or His Word?"

"God obviously came first," said his friend.

"Oh, was God dumb at the beginning and unable to speak?"

"No, He could speak," the friend insisted.

"Of course, because God is perfect. So at no time was He unable to speak and be without His Word. So Christ, the Word of God, has always been with God."

If at any point someone argues that Christians believe in three gods—God, Jesus, and Mary—you can show him that Jesus Himself said that God is one (Mark 12:29), and that the Towrah said the same thing (Deuteronomy 6:4).

The most difficult thing for a Muslim to believe is that Christ, who came in the flesh to our world, is the same God as the one God. This is because the theologians who were commentators of the Qur'an legitimately hated the idols that were worshiped along with God (Allah) many centuries ago. As a result, they fell in the trap of building their theology on the doctrine that God is a monolith who cannot be explained or defined because nothing is like Him. In this way they present God as unfree, unable to do what He wants or to appear to His creatures in the form He chooses.

Because of this error in thinking, we need to show our Muslim friends convincing examples, such as Christ being the Word of God who is always with God. Others are Christ's miraculous birth; His ability to create, and to heal diseases; and His ability to resurrect others and Himself from the grip of death. No sincere, clearthinking Muslim can deny what the Qur'an affirms about Christ's divine characteristics.

To further underscore the Word and the Spirit being one with God, go through the following verses with your friend:

## Readings

### Towrah

Micah 3:8 — "As for me [the Messiah], I am filled with power, with the Spirit of the LORD, and with justice and might, to declare to Jacob his transgression, to Israel his sin."

### Zabur

Psalm 139:7 — Where can I go from your Spirit? Where can I flee from your presence?

### Injeel

Revelation 19:13 — He is dressed in a robe dipped in blood, and his name is the Word of God.

Acts 20:28 — "Keep watch over yourselves and all the flock of which the Holy Spirit has made you overseers. Be shepherds of the church of God, which he bought with his own blood."

Here we see that God purchased believers with His own blood. Can God bleed? That shows the oneness of God, His Word, and His Spirit.

### Qur'an

Cow 2:87 — We [God] gave Jesus son of Mary the clear signs [miracles and God's words], and confirmed [sustained] him with the Holy Spirit.

In other words, God gave Jesus His words and sustained Him always with His Holy Spirit.

*

$I_s$ *Christ the Son of God?* This is an important question, but one that you should not pose to your friend, at least not right away. The Bible and the Qur'an speak of three kinds of sons:

1. *A physical son:* "Flesh gives birth to flesh" (John 3:6) speaks of a physical child being born from physical parents. Jesus was a physical person born of Mary, His physical mother. Because she was a virgin, He was without sin, according to the Qur'an (Mary 19:19)—"He [the angel] said, 'I am but a messenger come from thy Lord, to give thee a boy most pure [without sin]'"—and also the Bible (Hebrews 4:15), "We have one [a high priest, Christ] who has been tempted in every way, just as we are—yet was without sin."

In Sincere Religion 112:1-3 we read, "Say: 'He is God, One, God, the Everlasting Refuge, who has not begotten, and has not been begotten,'" which indicates that the phrase "Son of God" in relation to Christ is not intended in a physical sense, because God has no body. Certainly Christ's physical body is not God's body.

2. *A symbolic son:* Another usage of the word "son" (in the original languages of both the Qur'anic and biblical text) is the sense of belonging to. For example, "the son of the road" (Cow 2:177,215) means a traveler. The Injeel talks of "the sons of the light" (Luke 16:8), and the Zabur talks of "the son of wickedness" (Psalm 89:22, KJV). Obviously, the road, light, and wickedness do not literally have sons.

The Qur'an and the Bible use symbolic expressions to help us understand when they speak about God, also, as in these passages: "Glory be to Him, in whose hand is the dominion of everything" (Ya Sin 36:83); "The All-compassionate sat Himself upon the Throne" (Ta Ha 20:5); and "The eyes of the LORD range throughout the earth" (2 Chronicles 16:9). The terms "hand," "sat," and "eyes" help us understand God even though we know God has no body.

*3. A spiritual son:* The Injeel says, "Flesh gives birth to flesh, but the Spirit gives birth to spirit" (John 3:6), differentiating between a physical child and a spiritual child. In Women 4:171 we see that the son of Mary is from God: "The Messiah, Jesus son of Mary, was . . . the Messenger of God, and His Word that He committed to Mary, and a Spirit from Him." This says Jesus is God's Word from God and that He is also a Spirit from God. God is Spirit, and one who comes from—is "born of"—His Spirit is indeed Spirit.

But as the son of Mary, He is also human. The Injeel tells us in Hebrews 4:15 that Christ "has been tempted in every way, just as we are—yet was without sin."

The following passages from the Bible and the Qur'an indicate that God indeed had a Son, and they underscore the relationship between them.

## Readings

### Towrah

> Daniel 3:25 (KJV)—"The form of the fourth is like the Son of God."

This verse explains that a fourth person was clearly seen in the fiery furnace where three men of God—Shadrach, Meshach, and Abednego—were unjustly thrown. It seems that the fourth person protected the other three, and that it was none other than a pre-incarnational embodiment (a theophany) of Christ.

> Proverbs 30:4—"Who has gone up to heaven and come down? . . . What is his name, and the name of his son?"

## Zabur

Psalm 2:7-8—He [God] said to me [Christ], "You are my son. . . . Ask of me, and I will make the nations your inheritance, the ends of the earth your possession."

## Injeel

Matthew 3:16-17—As soon as Jesus was baptized, he went up out of the water. At that moment heaven was opened, and he saw the Spirit of God descending like a dove and lighting on him. And a voice from heaven said, "This is my Son, whom I love; with him I am well pleased."

Romans 1:3-4—Regarding his [God's] Son, who as to his human nature was a descendant of David, and who through the Spirit of holiness was declared with power to be the Son of God by his resurrection from the dead: Jesus Christ our Lord.

These verses and many others in the Injeel say that God's Son is Jesus Christ.

## Qur'an

Prophets 21:91—She [Mary] . . . guarded her virginity, so We [God] breathed into her of Our spirit and appointed her and her son to be a sign [miracle] unto all beings.

Cow 2:253—Those Messengers [prophets], some We [God] have preferred above others . . . some He raised in rank. And We [God] gave Jesus son of Mary the clear signs [miracles], and confirmed him with the Holy Spirit.

This verse lumps all the prophets together, but singles out Jesus as unique because of His miracles and the Holy Spirit in His life.

> Ant 27:8-9—When he [Moses] came to it, he was called: "Blessed is He who is in the fire, and he who is about it. Glory be to God, the Lord of all Being! Moses, behold, it is I, God, the All-mighty, the All-wise."

Some people say God could not be in a human being because that would be too limiting for Him. But here it says God inhabited fire (the burning bush Moses saw). How is it that God can exist in a bush and not be able to live in a pure human body?

✱

Neither Christ's life nor His miracles save us from our sins. Only His death and resurrection do this. Let's take a look at what Muslims believe about this.

They think Christ never died and never was resurrected. Instead, they believe He went to be with God directly. A literal reading of the Qur'an from the Arabic indicates that Christ will return to this world as "a sign that the last hour has come" (Ornaments 43:61). Traditions say Jesus will come back to earth, marry, have children, and lead the world to Islam. Then, after forty years, He will die and be buried in Medina next to Muhammad, in a tomb prepared there long ago. Then He will rise on Resurrection Day.

Here are some passages from the Qur'an that relate to Christ's death and resurrection:

## Readings

### Qur'an

> Cow 2:87—We [God] gave to Moses the Book . . . and We gave Jesus son of Mary the clear signs [miracles], and

confirmed [supported] him with the Holy Spirit; and whensoever there came to you a Messenger with that your souls had not desire for [something you didn't want], did you become arrogant, and some cry lies to [you called them liars, as was done to Moses and the Old Testament prophets], and some slay [referring to Jesus and the New Testament prophets]?

Table 5:120 — "I [Christ] was a witness [supervisor] over them [the people], while I remained among them; but when Thou [God] didst take me to Thyself [in death], Thou wast Thyself the watcher over them."

Mary 19:33-34 — "Peace be upon me [Christ], the day I was born, and the day I die, and the day I am raised up alive!" That is Jesus, son of Mary, in word of truth, concerning which they are doubting.

House of Imran 3:55 — God said, "Jesus, I will take thee to Me [in death] and will raise thee to Me, and I will purify thee of those who believe not [God will save Christ from them]. I will set thy followers above the unbelievers till the Resurrection Day."

The word "till" means until or before, indicating that all this will happen before Resurrection Day. Since Christ's followers exist now, this verse applies to the Easter events, not to Christ's return.

✳

But some Muslims will point to certain other passages from the Qur'an to counter any claims about the Crucifixion. For example, they might point out Women 4:157: "They did not slay him, neither crucified him, only a likeness of that was shown to them [it only seemed that way]." Many Muslims use this verse to point out that the Qur'an says Jesus didn't die.

But the text here must be examined in the broader context. In Women 4, the Qur'an relates how the Jews and Christians were arguing. The Jews were essentially boasting, "We killed your false Messiah," trying to persuade Muhammad that their way was right and that the Christian way was wrong. But Muhammad puts the Jews down in Women 4:157, saying, "Don't say that you killed Him. You didn't. It just looked that way." For the Jews had no authority to kill anyone; it was the *Romans* who killed Jesus. But the Jews were ultimately responsible for the crucifixion of Jesus.

The Jewish way of killing was stoning, anyway. But this kind of death would have made Jesus a martyr, which they didn't want. So they provoked the Romans to do it by the Roman method: crucifixion. In this way, Jesus was cursed according to Jewish law: "Anyone who is hung on a tree is under God's curse" (Deuteronomy 21:23).

God could have protected Jesus. But He let it happen. Something similar happened at the Muslim victory at Badr. In Spoils 8:17 it says, "You [the believers] did not slay them, but God slew them; and when thou threwest [arrows], it was not thyself that threw, but God threw." In other words, God did the killing through those shooting arrows to accomplish His purpose.

In the same way God permitted the Roman soldiers to kill Christ in order to ransom us with a "mighty sacrifice" (Rangers 37:107). Not with a ram or camel or even five hundred beasts, as some commentators have claimed, but with the Word of God Himself.

Have all these stories in your mind as you witness. Have the verses on cards. Like a good blacksmith, you beat and beat the metal. The more you use these verses, the more effective will be your witness.

When Christ was dead and properly buried in a sealed tomb, the Jewish leaders felt relieved. They had finally freed themselves from the criticism of their own hypocrisy, double-faced living, and exploitation of the simple people. But it was short-lived. "The All-mighty, All-wise God has raised him up" (Women 4:158). God nullified their plans for getting rid of Him. He defeated their plot and resurrected Christ from the dead.

The real point you need to drive home to your friend is that the essential step in our sin dilemma had to be taken by God. What is important is not what man did but what *God* did—in Christ. The following passages from the Bible and the Qur'an address that dimension of Principle 5.

## Readings

### Towrah

> Isaiah 63:4-5—"The year of my redemption has come. I looked, but there was no one to help, I was appalled that no one gave support; so my own arm worked salvation for me."

> Ezekiel 36:25-26—"I will cleanse you from all your impurities and from all your idols. I will give you a new heart and put a new spirit in you; I will remove from you your heart of stone and give you a heart of flesh."

> Isaiah 53:12—He [the coming Christ] poured out his life unto death, and was numbered with the transgressors. For he bore the sin of many, and made intercession for the transgressors.

### Zabur

> Psalm 106:8—He saved them for his name's sake.

> Psalm 41:4—"O LORD, have mercy on me; heal me, for I have sinned against you."

> Psalm 103:2-4—Praise the LORD, O my soul . . . who forgives all your sins . . . who redeems your life from the pit.

## Injeel

Hebrews 9:22 — The law requires that nearly everything be cleansed with blood, and without the shedding of blood there is no forgiveness.

1 Timothy 2:5-6 — Christ Jesus . . . gave himself as a ransom for all men.

1 Corinthians 15:3-4 — What I received I passed on to you as of first importance: that Christ died for our sins according to the Scriptures, that he was buried, that he was raised on the third day according to the Scriptures.

Hebrews 2:3 — How shall we escape if we neglect so great a salvation [of Christ]?

Luke 9:25 — "What good is it for a man to gain the whole world, and yet lose or forfeit his very self?"

## Qur'an

Cattle 6:12 — "He [God] has prescribed for Himself mercy [it has been written regarding Himself to be merciful]."

Hood 11:43 — Said he [Noah], "Today there is no defender from God's command but for him on whom He has mercy."

Believers 23:109 — "There is a party of My servants who said, 'Our Lord, we believe; therefore forgive us, and have mercy on us, for Thou art the best of the merciful.'"

God is indeed merciful to give us His Word to die for us, as well as His Spirit. What greater mercy could there be than to go to this extreme sacrifice?

Pilgrimage 22:36-37 — And the beasts of sacrifice . . . the flesh of them shall not reach God, neither their blood, but godliness from you shall reach Him.

Jesus has taken the place of all those old sacrifices that are still being offered today on Mount Arafat in Saudi Arabia. The air is filled with the putrefaction of these sacrifices because people do not know how to make use of them due to their large number. Other people try to replace these sacrifices today with good works. But ultimately none of this will have significance to God. He wants "godliness." But what *is* true godliness?

Tradition says Muhammad told his daughter not to forget to put her hand on the head of a sacrificed animal, so that when it was killed, she would be identified with it. He understood well the need for a sacrifice for our sins. And what did he consider to be real godliness or righteousness?

The word "Islam" means submission to God's will, which should mean to us turning our face toward God and accepting His plan of salvation for our lives. The word *godliness* means fearing God and accepting what He is doing for us. If we accept what He has done for us at the Cross, then *His* righteousness is applied to our account and thus becomes ours.

After we recognize the vital importance of what God did for us, we must reckon with what is an appropriate response on our part. So, make an appointment with your friend to discuss the next principle.

# CHAPTER 14
# PRINCIPLE SIX:
# Making Him Ours

After we realize the wonder and the power of God's gift of Himself to us, our minds are boggled. We respond by asking ourselves, "What then should we do? How can this salvation from God become truly ours?" The answer is found in Principle 6: *We must invite Christ, our substitute, to live in our hearts and be the master of our lives.* Here are some passages from the Bible and the Qur'an that help explain this concept.

## Readings

### Towrah

> Jeremiah 24:7—"I will give them a heart to know me, that I am the LORD. They will be my people, and I will be their God, for they will return to me with all their heart."

### Zabur

> Psalm 13:5—I trust in your unfailing love; my heart rejoices in your salvation.

## Injeel

> Revelation 3:20 — "Here I am! I stand at the door and knock. If anyone hears my voice and opens the door, I will come in and eat with him, and he with me."

## Qur'an

> Thunder 13:27-29 — "He [God] guides to Him all who are penitent." Those who believe, their hearts being at rest in God's remembrance [that is, when you think of God, trust Him and surrender to Him]—in God's remembrance are at rest the hearts of those who believe and do righteous deeds; theirs is blessedness and a fair resort [a good end].

What good news! God will guide the repentant. Imagine that— repenting and believing will lead our hearts to be at rest. We should obey God and receive by faith the Person—Christ—whom He has appointed as Savior, Redeemer, and Mediator, both in this world and in the world to come. Ask your friend to say a simple prayer asking God to clean his heart and to help him live with that kind of repentance and faith forever. Discuss with your friend the meaning of the terms *Savior*, *Redeemer*, and *Mediator*.

✳

A man wanted to climb to a high mountain peak. He brought all the necessary equipment and hired a seasoned guide to show him the way. As they started, conditions were perfect. They stopped for a light lunch, then started off again. The small path that they were following soon disappeared. Rugged cliffs loomed everywhere.

Suddenly they came to a deep gorge. The guide approached the edge and examined it. He found a sturdy rock and, after testing it, jumped from it to the other side. The other man wanted to follow him, but every time he got ready, his fear of falling to his death kept him from jumping.

So, the guide tied himself to a rock, planted his feet firmly in the ground, and stretched his arm out toward the man. He told him to hold on to his hand tightly and then jump. The man still hesitated in fear. The guide looked him right in the eye and said, "Sir, this hand has helped many climbers across this very passage, and it hasn't failed a single one. Trust in it, and jump over!"

The climber jumped. All at once, there he was on the other side, safe and full of joy that he was on his way again to the top of the mountain.

We, also, are on the path to a very high summit, leading us to the peace of God and His eternal life. We have to reckon with the question of whether we are refusing or hesitating to trust ourselves to His divine hand to help us. We need to trust in that hand, wounded for us on the Cross, letting Him save us. Ask your friend who the guide represents. The following verses in the Bible and the Qur'an speak of our desperate need to risk reaching out for the steady, reliable hand of God, which is already reaching out to us.

## Readings

### Towrah

1 Chronicles 22:19 — "Now devote [set] your heart and soul to seeking the LORD your God."

Ezekiel 18:31-32 — "Rid yourselves of all the offenses you have committed, and get a new heart and a new spirit. Why will you die? . . . For I take no pleasure in the death of anyone, declares the Sovereign LORD. Repent and live!"

## Zabur

Psalm 119:145,149—I call with all my heart; answer me,
O LORD. . . . Hear my voice in accordance with your love;
preserve my life, O LORD, according to your laws.

Psalm 28:7—The LORD is my strength and my shield; my
heart trusts in him, and I am helped. My heart leaps for joy.

## Injeel

Romans 10:10—It is with your heart that you believe and
are justified, and it is with your mouth that you confess and
are saved.

Hebrews 10:22-23—Let us draw near to God with a
sincere heart in full assurance of faith, having our hearts
sprinkled to cleanse us from a guilty conscience. . . . Let us
hold unswervingly to the hope we profess, for he who
promised is faithful.

## Qur'an

Disputer 58:22—He [God] has written faith upon their
hearts, and He has confirmed them with a Spirit from
Himself.

God is the only one who gives faith. If He doesn't, we will never
have it. The Qur'an does not even mention good works here.
When a man receives Christ in faith, God puts the Holy Spirit in
him. That is the meaning of "He has confirmed them with a Spirit
from Himself."

Mutual Fraud 64:11—Whosoever believes in God, He will
guide his heart. And God has knowledge of everything.

In other words, God will guide whoever believes in Him.

> Women 4:110—Whoever does evil, or wrongs himself,
> and then prays God's forgiveness, he shall find God is All-
> forgiving, All-compassionate.

It is obvious in this verse that God will not cast anyone outside
who comes to Him in repentance.

✳

The following story illustrates how one Western Christian in the
Middle East applied Principle 6. When Israel invaded southern
Lebanon in 1978, relief agencies gave great amounts of food for
distribution to those suffering from the war. Haleem, a Palestinian
young man, brought his friends to the office of Sam, who was
engaged in this relief distribution, to ask for help in repackaging
the food into family-size bundles for refugees. Haleem felt comfortable inviting his friends there because he had previously studied the Bible and some of the Seven Principles with Sam.

Because Haleem was quite reserved and would not open up
quickly to new people, it was hard at first for Sam to even carry
on a conversation with him. But Haleem showed genuine interest
in the Bible. In fact, he had already had informal Bible study with
other friends who had left the Middle East four years prior to this.

For a week Sam worked six or seven hours a day with Haleem
and a Palestinian friend of his in shacks where the trucks dumped
the food. For one family they would assemble a package of rice,
sugar, powdered milk, canned meat, lentils, soap, and a few other
things. Then they would deliver the packages to refugee sites.

This experience cemented Sam's relationship with Haleem,
who saw Sam care so much for the plight of his people. At last
Sam saw a breakthrough in the friendship. Then Haleem began
to take the initiative to invite Sam to some event, or he would go
see him spontaneously out of pure friendship.

It was at this point that they read through Principle 6 together.

Afterwards, Sam told Haleem how he had become a believer and what he had prayed on that eventful day. He went on talking.

Two minutes later Haleem said, "Would you repeat that?" Sam repeated what he had just said. "No," said Haleem, "would you repeat that prayer?" Sam did. "I would like to pray that, too," said Haleem.

Haleem was quite sensitive to the plight of his people. Seeing Sam get involved in meeting their need opened up his heart to what Sam had to share. The truth *plus* relentless love had a powerful effect.

God has done His part for the salvation of our lives. The question at hand is, Have we done *our* part? Schedule a time to meet with your friend to discuss Principle 7, which focuses on what we receive when we have united with God through faith in Christ.

## CHAPTER 15
# PRINCIPLE SEVEN:
# What to Expect When We Accept God's Gift

After someone truly takes the sixth step to embrace Christ, what can he expect? The final step deals with what happens after all the other steps are taken. The fruit of the other steps can be understood in Principle 7: *When we accept Christ, we receive forgiveness for our sins, a personal relationship with God, peace in our hearts, and a complete change in our lives.* This change in what we *are*, what we *do*, and how we *live* is reflected in certain passages in the Bible and the Qur'an.

## Readings

### Towrah

> Ezekiel 36:26-27—"I will give you a new heart and put a new spirit in you; I will remove from you your heart of stone and give you a heart of flesh. And I will put my Spirit in you and move you to follow my decrees and be careful to keep my laws."

## Zabur

Psalm 119:162-165—I rejoice in your promise like one who finds great spoil. . . . Seven times a day I praise you for your righteous laws. Great peace have they who love your law, and nothing can make them stumble.

## Injeel

John 1:12-13—Yet to all who received him [Christ, "the Word"], to those who believed in his name, he gave the right to become children of God—children born not of natural descent, nor of human decision or a husband's will, but born of God.

## Qur'an

Believers 40:2-3—God the All-mighty, the All-knowing, Forgiver of sins, Accepter of penitence, Terrible in retribution.

God is almighty and He can give everything we need. He forgives and accepts us, but if we are not coming to Him, we are under His judgment, and it is terrible.

We need to be convinced that we are dependent on God's help to receive salvation and the full life He has for us now and forever. You should make sure that your Muslim friend is also convinced that the divine Person appointed by God to be our Redeemer and Savior is His mighty Word, anointed by His eternal Spirit. You can let your friend know that when we believe in Christ and invite Him to enter our hearts to rule over our lives, then we will receive the following:

◆ Forgiveness for all our past sins, and also God's help to enable us to resist temptation and sin in the future. (You may want to read some of these passages together: Psalms 32:5, 103:8-13; Proverbs 28:13; Isaiah 43:25, 53:1-7; Ezekiel 36:25; Micah 7:18-20; Matthew 9:1-8; Romans 5:6-9; Ephesians 2:1-10.)

◆ A fresh, personal relationship with God in which He favors us and delights to give us His divine treasures of blessing. (See Psalm 16:7-11, Jeremiah 31:34, Romans 8:12-17, Hebrews 10:12-18, 1 Peter 1:3-5, 1 John 3:1-24.)

◆ Perfect peace of mind and assurance that our names have been written in heaven to receive eternal life with God. (See Psalm 4:8; Isaiah 26:3, 43:1-3; John 6:47-51, 10:22-30, 14:27; Romans 5:1-11; Philippians 4:6-7; 1 John 5:11-13; Revelation 3:1-5.)

◆ A new love for God and a desire to live as He wants, as well as a distaste for old sins in your life and the power to leave them behind. (See Ezekiel 36:26-31, 2 Corinthians 5:14-21, Colossians 3:1-14.)

If your Muslim friend wants these incredible gifts in his life and believes that Christ, God's Word, is God's provision for his salvation, then it would probably be quite appropriate for you to offer the following prayer or perhaps one of your own words to your friend as a way to seal his relationship with God in Jesus Christ.

## Prayer for Salvation

I come to You, oh Creator of the universe, with great respect. I have turned my back on You, choosing to do wrong, resulting in despair and darkness in my life. But I am bold to come to You now because I know that You love me. I want to accept Christ, Your Word, who took the punishment for my sins when He gave Himself for me on the cross as a ransom and then rose from the grave, and now prays for me at Your right-hand side.

As I now surrender myself to You through Christ, I trust You to give me eternal life, peace of mind, and a heart that will obey You and reject sin. Thank You for hearing me. Amen.

As you can see, we used almost all verses from the Bible in Principle 7. By now your friend understands enough so you don't have to use many verses from the Qur'an, which has served its purpose as a bridge to the truth. But in case you feel that your friend still needs a few more verses, you may find those listed at the end of this chapter to be helpful.

If your friend has sincerely prayed this prayer of commitment to Christ and acceptance of Christ, if you feel it is appropriate you might want to type up a statement for him to sign to document and serve as a record of the when and what of this important decision. It might look something like this:

I, _____,
(name)

**gave my whole life to Christ Jesus**

**to be my personal Savior and Lord on**

_____
(date)

# How to Strengthen One's Relationship with God

1. Encourage your friend to decide on a quiet place and time each day to read and think about the Scriptures in order to hear God speak to him. If he cannot do this, mention that he should grab any time or place available to do it.

2. Let your friend know that before reading the Scriptures, he should ask God to help him understand what he reads. After reading, he should ask God to help him believe and obey what he has read.

3. Encourage your friend to confess to God each specific sin and shortcoming that he has committed since his last reading, and to ask God to forgive him and help him not to do it again.

4. Let your friend know the importance of seeking opportunities to be with other believers in Christ. A hot coal alone cools quickly, but a hot coal among other hot coals remains hot. Reassure him that it is only right for him to pray with other believers and to study God's Word together since they have become his spiritual family.

5. Unless it would be extremely divisive, your friend should be telling his friends and family about God's love, urging them to leave their bad ways and to seek God for help so that they too can have eternal life. If this seems impossible at first, get your friend to pray to Almighty God very earnestly for them and to trust God with their lives. He is the God of the impossible. Then he just needs to continue to love, help, and respect them more than ever before, emphasizing to them clearly that he is not leaving them or following another religion. The point is that he has simply accepted in his life Christ, the Word of God, as Savior and Intercessor. If they are interested and willing to

dialogue, then he should show them from all the passages he has learned in both the Bible and the Qur'an that God has sent Christ to save everybody in the world and to give them eternal life and happiness.

## Passages from the Qur'an

House of Imran 3:134-135—God loves the good-doers; who, when they commit an indecency or wrong themselves, remember God, and pray forgiveness for their sins—and who shall forgive sins but God?—and do not persevere in the things they did and that wittingly.

Note in this passage how God forgave these repentant people all their past sins and gave them power to conquer future weaknesses and disobedience.

House of Imran 3:42-49—And when the Angels said, "Mary, God has chosen thee, and purified thee; He has chosen thee above all women. Mary, be obedient to thy Lord, prostrating and bowing before Him." ... "God gives thee good tidings of a Word from Him whose name is Messiah, Jesus, son of Mary; high honoured shall he be in this world and the next, near stationed to God ... and righteous he shall be." ... "And He [God] will teach him [Christ] the Book, the Wisdom, the Torah, the Gospel, to be a Messenger ... saying, 'I have come to you with a sign from your Lord. I will create for you out of clay as the likeness of a bird; then I will breathe into it, and it will be a bird, by the leave of God. I will also heal the blind and the leper, and bring to life the dead, by the leave of God. I will inform you too of what things you eat, and what you treasure up in your houses. Surely in that is a sign for you, if you are believers.'"

Note the special personal relationship and perfect peace of mind the Virgin Mary had with God because she believed in His Word and trusted Him completely for her future life.

> House of Imran 3:52-53 — And when Jesus perceived their [the Jews'] unbelief, he said, "Who will be my helpers unto God?" The Apostles said, "We will be helpers of God; we believe in God; witness thou our submission. Lord, we believe in that Thou hast sent down, and we follow the Messenger. Inscribe us therefore with those who bear witness."

Note here that the followers of Christ believed in God and were God's helpers. They were in God's peace and their names were written in heaven where the names of the righteous are written.

> Cattle 6:126-127 — This is the path of thy Lord; straight; We have distinguished the signs to a people who remember. Theirs is the abode of peace with their Lord, and He is their Protector for that they were doing.

Note that those who obey God will be in the Lord's presence, a home of peace, and He will be their friend — all because they have accepted God's plan to become righteous.

> Cattle 6:122 — Why, is he who was dead, and We gave him life, and appointed for him a light to walk by among the people as one whose likeness is in the shadows, and comes not forth from them?

Note the difference between those who were dead in their sins, then accepted life from God and decided to walk in His light, and those who refused to accept God's mercy and remained in their shadows of darkness.

Counsel 42:9—God . . . is the Protector; He quickens the dead, and He is powerful over everything.

Note that God is the only protector who can give life to all those who are dead in sin because He is powerful over everything. In order to receive this eternal life, sinners have to repent, ask God's pardon, and follow His plan of salvation.

House of Imran 3:55—When God said, "Jesus, I will take thee to Me and will raise thee to Me, and I will purify thee of those who believe not. I will set thy followers above the unbelievers till the Resurrection Day."

Note God's plan to help people believe in Him and receive His blessings and eternal life. It is through Christ's death and their act of following Him that they will come out from the ranks of the unbelievers and the disobedients to be with Him always after the Resurrection Day.

# CHAPTER 16
# Does the Qur'an Support Jesus' Crucifixion?

❦

After Muhammad died, some interpreters of the Qur'an said there was a substitute for Christ on the cross. They interpret Women 4:157, which says, "They did not slay him, neither crucified him, only a likeness of that was shown to them," to mean that Christ was not crucified but that someone else miraculously replaced Him on the cross. But the subject of the sentence is the Jews, and indeed, the Jews themselves did *not* crucify Jesus.

By changing one Arabic word in the final phrase in this sentence, which would literally be translated "it seemed to them so" (Arabic: *Shubbiha lahum*), and replacing it with *Shubbiha bihi*, which would be translated "in him," the meaning is changed to "someone who resembled Christ appeared to people (on the cross)." This alteration of the Qur'an leads to the common interpretation, which is: It *seemed* to them that Christ was on the cross, but He really was not.

But the following verse, Women 4:158, goes on to say, "God raised him [Jesus] up to Him." God would not raise up Jesus if He were not dead. The following Qur'anic verses support Christ's death.

Spider 29:46—Dispute not with the People of the Book [Christians] save in the fairer [kind] manner, except for those of them that do wrong; and say, "We believe in what has been sent down to us [the Qur'an], and what has been sent down to you [the Bible]; our God and your God is One, and to Him we have surrendered."

That is, Muslims and Christians believe in the same God, and have surrendered to Him. This verse also seems to say that the Qur'an should not contradict the Bible.

Cow 2:136—Say you: "We believe in God, and in that which has been sent down on us [the Qur'an] and sent down on Abraham, Ishmael, Isaac and Jacob, and the Tribes, and that which was given to Moses and Jesus and the Prophets, of their Lord [that is, the Bible]; we make no division between any of them, and to Him we surrender."

This passage says explicitly that the Bible was sent down from God and that Muslims believe in it. This very Bible states clearly that Christ was crucified for our sins, and so in effect Muslims are here told to believe in it. Here also the Qur'an says Muslims are to make no division, but to surrender to God in the way that the Bible teaches them.

Poets 26:192-197—Truly it [the Qur'an] is the revelation of the Lord of all Being, brought down by the Faithful Spirit upon thy heart [referring to Muhammad], that thou mayest be one of the warners, in a clear, Arabic tongue. Truly it is in the Scriptures of the ancients [the Scriptures of Jews and Christians who came before]. Was it not a sign [a proof] for them, that it [the Qur'an] is known to the learned of the Children of Israel?

In other words, the Qur'an was given to Muhammad to warn the Arabs in Arabic (because they could not understand the Old Testament in Hebrew or the New Testament in Greek). And Muhammad says that what he is teaching Muslims is known to the Jews. Therefore, the Qur'an commands Muslims not to contradict the Jews and Christians due to the stated principle that the Qur'an agrees with the Scriptures of both Jews and Christians.

Each of these passages urges Muslims not to contradict what the Towrah, Zabur, and Injeel say. Some ancient and respected commentators and writers of *hadith* (Muslim tradition) disagree with how modern interpreters should handle Women 4:157. Az Zamakhshari, Ar Razi, Ibn Abbas, Wahab, Muhammad Ibn Ishaak, and others say that Christ remained dead for some three to seven hours before being raised to heaven by God. The story of a substitute on the cross is contradictory and untrue for the following reasons:

- ◆ At least ten different people have been proposed as the substitute, from Christ's best friends (John and Peter) to his worst enemies (Judas), or completely neutral persons (the man Simon who bore the cross). Some even say Satan was Christ's substitute on the cross, for how could such a good person as Christ be killed and crucified? Muslims are taught that God would not allow His prophet to be killed, so they say God substituted someone on the cross, deceiving all of us as to who it was. But most of the prophets have been killed, as the Qur'an also says.

- ◆ It is inconceivable that God, the Wise and Almighty, should adopt such a miracle of falsity in order to deceive the Jews (and everyone else) and let them cause the wrong person to be killed.

- ◆ In Cow 2:253 and several other places we read that God "confirmed [Jesus as the Christ] with the Holy Spirit." It was part of God's plan for Christ to die. Remember God rescuing Abraham's son with a mighty sacrifice? God wanted to rescue us with the mighty sacrifice of His Incarnate Word as payment for our sin. Couldn't God's Spirit enable Christ to go through with the Crucifixion? Couldn't God carry His program through to the end?

◆ The Qur'an indicates that Christ could raise the dead. If He was so powerful, why would God have to pull a trick? Since God Himself planned for Christ to die, how could all these people be so strong as to be able to keep Christ from dying? All a Muslim's life he is taught that it is so unreasonable for Christ to die. Now you need to show how truly unreasonable it would be for God to pull a trick and make it merely look like Christ died.

◆ Since God was fully able to raise Christ from the grave, it was unnecessary to kill an innocent substitute in His place.

◆ Why wouldn't this alleged substitute make any effort to defend himself, to declare that he was not the Christ? Surely something would have been heard of this if it had occurred.

◆ Those who were most devoted to Christ told people more than any others that they had seen Him suffer the death of a criminal at the hands of the Roman soldiers. Surely they, of all people, would have preferred that He finish His life in a manner that they would think suitable for a prophet—by direct removal to heaven.

And so it seems clear that not only does the Qur'an support the historical fact of Jesus' crucifixion but pure logic supports it. Help your friend see that the Cross and the Resurrection are inextricably linked together.

# CHAPTER 17

# The Bible Was Not Corrupted

᭟

Another thorny issue that often comes up in religious dialogue with Muslims is the belief that the Bible (the Towrah plus the Zabur plus the Injeel) that we have now is not like the original version. However, there is overwhelming evidence to prove quite the contrary.

## What Does the Qur'an Say About the Towrah?

Here are some passages from the Qur'an that will help your Muslim friend see a very respectful view of the Towrah (the Old Testament).

> Cow 2:87—"We [God] gave to Moses the Book [the Old Testament], and after him sent succeeding Messengers [the Jewish Prophets]."

In other words, Moses represents the authors of all the Old Testament Scriptures.

> Hobbling 45:16—Indeed, We [God] gave the Children of Israel the Book [the Old Testament], the Judgment

[discernment of good and evil and all the law], and the Prophethood [knowing things before they happen], and We provided them [the Jews] with good things, and We preferred them above all beings.

Prostration 32:23-24—Indeed, We [God] gave Moses the Book [the Old Testament]; so be not in doubt concerning the encounter with him [God's encounter with Moses]; and We appointed it for a guidance to the Children of Israel. And We appointed from among them leaders guiding by Our command, when they [the leaders] endured patiently, and had sure faith in Our signs.

We see here that Moses talked to God face-to-face. He knew the Source where he was getting his information.

Women 4:54—We [God] gave the people of Abraham [the Jews] the Book and the Wisdom, and We gave them a mighty kingdom.

Believers 40:53-54—We also gave Moses the guidance, and We bequeathed upon the Children of Israel the Book for a guidance and for a reminder [to remember what God had done for them] to men possessed of minds [not fools, but men with a holy intelligence].

## What Does the Qur'an Say About the Zabur?
Next take a look at what the Qur'an specifically says about the Zabur (the Psalms).

Women 4:163—We [God] gave to David Psalms.

Prophets 21:105—We have written in the Psalms, after the Remembrance [the Old and New Testaments], "The earth shall be the inheritance of My righteous servants."

## What Does the Qur'an Say About the Injeel?

Now here are some verses you can use as a resource to show your friend what the Qur'an says about the Injeel (the New Testament).

> Iron 57:27—And We sent, following [the Old Testament prophets], Jesus son of Mary, and gave unto him the Gospel. And We set in the hearts of those who followed him tenderness and mercy. And monasticism they invented—We did not prescribe it for them—only seeking the good pleasure of God.

> Table 5:49—And We sent, following in their footsteps [the Old Testament prophets], Jesus son of Mary, confirming the Torah before him; and We gave to him the Gospel, wherein is guidance and light, and confirming the Torah before it, as a [book of] guidance and an admonition unto the godfearing.

> Ornaments 43:63—And when Jesus came with the clear signs he said, "I have come to you with wisdom, and that I may make clear to you some of that whereon you are at variance; so fear you God and obey you me."

## What Does the Qur'an Say About Itself?

We have seen what the Qur'an says about the Bible. Just what does it say about itself?

> Cattle 6:92—This is a Book [the Qur'an] We have sent down, blessed and confirming [supporting] that which was before it [the Bible].

> Table 5:51—We have sent down to thee the Book [the Qur'an] with the truth, confirming the Book that was before it [the Bible], and assuring it.

Jonah 10:37—This Koran could not have been forged [made] apart from [without] God; but it is a confirmation of what is before it [the Towrah, Zabur, and Injeel—in other words, the Bible], and a distinguishing [listing the details] of the Book [the Bible], wherein is no doubt [which is without doubt], from the Lord of all Being.

Angels 35:31—And that We have revealed to thee [Muhammad] of the Book [in heaven] is the truth, confirming what is before it [the Bible].

Joseph 12:111—It [what the Qur'an relates] is not a tale forged, but a confirmation of what is before it [the Bible].

## What Does the Qur'an Say About Muhammad?

Your Muslim friend may want to know how Muhammad is referred to specifically in the Qur'an in relation to the Towrah, Zabur, and Injeel. Here are some passages that may give some perspective.

Poets 26:192-199—Truly it [the Qur'an] is the revelation of the Lord of all Being, brought down by the Faithful Spirit upon thy heart [Muhammad], that thou mayest be one of the warners, in a clear, Arabic tongue. Truly it [the Qur'an] is in the Scriptures [the Bible] of the ancients [it is not something new]. Was it not a sign [proof] for them, that it is known to the learned [knowledgeable] of the Children of Israel? If We [God] had sent it down on a barbarian [a non-Arab] and he had recited it to them, they would not have believed in it [for lack of understanding its language].

Jonah 10:94—So, if thou [Muhammad] art in doubt regarding what We have sent down [the Qur'an] to thee, ask those who recite the Book [the Bible] before thee. The truth has come to thee from thy Lord; so be not of the doubters.

## What Did Muhammad's Jewish and Christian Contemporaries Think of the Qur'an?

Using the following passages from the Qur'an itself as your resource, you can give your Muslim friend a sense of what Muhammad's Jewish and Christian contemporaries thought of the Qur'an.

Cow 2:91 — And when they [the Jews] were told, "Believe in that God has sent down [the Qur'an]," they said, "We believe in what was sent down on us [the Old Testament]"; and they disbelieve in what is beyond that [the New Testament and the Qur'an], yet it is the truth confirming what is with them [the Old Testament].

Cow 2:101 — When there has come to them [Jews and Christians] a Messenger from God confirming what was with them [the Bible], a party of them that were given the Book [the Bible] reject the Book of God [the Qur'an] behind their backs, as though they knew [it] not.

Cow 2:89 — When there came to them [the Jews] a Book from God [the Qur'an], confirming what was with them [the Old Testament] . . . they disbelieved in it.

Cow 2:40-41 — Children of Israel, remember My blessing wherewith I [God] blessed you [Jews], and fulfil My covenant and I shall fulfil your covenant . . . and believe in that I have sent down [the Qur'an], confirming that which is with you [the Old Testament], and be not the first to disbelieve in it.

In the following passages from the Qur'an, Muhammad says those who follow the teaching of their own Scriptures do not need anything else.

Table 5:46-47 — Yet how will they [the Jews] make thee [Muhammad] their judge seeing they have the Torah, wherein is God's judgment? . . . Surely We sent down the Torah, wherein is guidance and light; thereby the Prophets who had surrendered themselves [to God] gave judgment for those of Jewry, as did the masters [Jewish teachers] and the rabbis, following such portion of God's Book [the Old Testament] as they were given to keep and were witnesses to [follow]. So [everyone] fear not men, but fear you Me; and sell not My signs [miracles and verses of a revealed Book] for a little price. Whoso judges not according to what God has sent down [to him]—they are the unbelievers.

Table 5:50—So let the People of the Gospel [Christians] judge according to [follow] what God has sent down therein. Whosoever judges not according to what God has sent down—they are the ungodly.

Table 5:72—Surely they that believe, and those of Jewry, and the Sabaeans [probably John the Baptist's followers], and those Christians, whoever believes in God and the Last Day, and works righteousness—no fear shall be on them, neither shall they sorrow.

House of Imran 3:113-114—Some of the People of the Book [the Bible] are a nation upstanding, that recite God's signs [God's Word, the Bible] in the watches of the night, bowing themselves, believing in God and in the Last Day, bidding to honour and forbidding dishonour, vying [competing] one with the other in good works; those are the righteous. [Muhammad may have been describing here what he saw in some Christian monasteries when he visited them.]

Table 5:85-86—Thou wilt surely find the nearest of them in love to the believers [Muslims] are those who say "We

are Christians"; that, because some of them are priests and
monks, and they wax not proud, and when they hear what
has been sent down [the Qur'an] to the Messenger
[Muhammad], thou seest their eyes overflow with tears
because of the truth they recognize.

In fact, the Qur'an says no one can be a good Muslim unless he
practices the teachings of the Towrah, Zabur, and Injeel:

Women 4:136—O believers [Muslims], believe in God
and His Messenger [Muhammad] and the Book [the
Qur'an] He has sent down on His Messenger [the passage
could have ended here, but . . .] and the Book [the Bible]
which He sent down before. Whoso disbelieves in God
and His angels and His Books, and His Messengers [all
of them], and the Last Day, has surely gone astray into
far error.

House of Imran 3:84—Say [spoken to Muhammad], "We
believe in God, and that which has been sent down on us
[the Qur'an], and sent down on Abraham and Ishmael,
Isaac and Jacob, and the Tribes [the Old Testament], and
in that which was given to Moses and Jesus, and the
Prophets, of their Lord [the Bible]; we make no division
between any of them, and to Him we surrender."

Cow 2:136—Say you [spoken to Muslims]: "We believe in
God, and in that which has been sent down on us and sent
down on Abraham, Ishmael, Isaac and Jacob, and the
Tribes, and that which was given to Moses and Jesus and
the Prophets, of their Lord; we make no division between
any of them, and to Him we surrender."

Cow 2:285—The Messenger [Muhammad] believes in
what was sent down to him [the Qur'an] from his Lord,

and the believers [Muslims]; each one believes in God and His angels, and in His Books and His Messengers; we make no division between any one of His Messengers.

Spider 29:46 — Dispute [argue] not with the People of the Book [Jews and Christians] save in the fairer [gentle] manner, except for those of them that do wrong; and say, "We [Muslims] believe in what has been sent down to us [Qur'an], and what has been sent down to you [the Bible]; our God and your God is One, and to Him we [all] have surrendered."

Table 5:71 — Say: "People of the Book [Muslims here], you do not stand on anything, until you perform the Torah and the Gospel, and what [the Qur'an] was sent down to you [Muslims] from your Lord." [That is, the Muslim also is called to obey the Bible.]

Obviously these verses show that Muhammad did not think the Bible was corrupted in his time. Has it been corrupted since then, since the seventh century A.D.? Consider these points:

Long before Muhammad's lifetime and to this very day, the Jews were sharply divided over many issues, resulting in the development of various separate Jewish groups. In the same way, Christians since the first century have differed greatly in religious beliefs, resulting in scores of different denominations. Many times Muhammad referred to these divisions in the Qur'an. For example, in Cow 2:253 he said, "Had God willed, those who came after him [Christ] would not have fought one against the other after the clear signs [the clear message of Christ] had come to them; but they fell into variance, and some of them believed, and some disbelieved."

Before Christ's time the Towrah and Zabur existed in Hebrew, Greek, and partly in Aramaic. Also, before Muhammad's time at least part of the Bible existed in these additional languages — Syriac, Coptic, Latin, Armenian, and Gothic.

In order for the Bible to be corrupted after Muhammad's time, the following events would have had to happen:

1.  Representatives from every Jewish and Christian sect and denomination from at least seven or eight nations and languages, who were fighting with each other over controversial theological issues, would have needed to hold a conference and agree in detail on an explosive issue, namely, the changing of their Scriptures. (Of course, each sect would have wanted to change it to support the particular beliefs that split them in the first place.)
2.  They would have had to agree on how to issue their new, corrupted version of the Bible.
3.  They would have had to convince everyone who had a Bible in any language to exchange it for a new, corrupted version.
4.  All the original Bibles would have had to be destroyed, leaving no evidence to succeeding generations.

If indeed these events did happen, then who can supply the date and place of such a conference and name the participants and their resolutions? Historical records before Muhammad's time of events of far less importance exist. Thus it is highly unlikely that there is documented evidence to validate such a history-changing event. In addition, manuscripts exist from long before Muhammad's birth that agree with current translations of the Bible.

In fact, Muhammad himself seems to have foreseen such erroneous beliefs:

Jonah 10:64—There is no changing the words of God; that is the mighty triumph.

Cattle 6:34—No man can change the words of God.

Angels 35:43 — Thou shalt never find any changing the wont [will] of God, and thou shalt never find any altering the wont of God.

Some of the passages from the Qur'an in this chapter will help your friend see that both Muhammad and the Qur'an are on the side of the authority of the Bible. There are also passages stating not only that God wanted the Bible to exist but that the Bible has not been tampered with. This is a reassuring concept to someone who might very well have a latent fear that what he has just come to believe in through your guidance contains errors and is disapproved of by his Muslim family and friends. But the Qur'an is clearly on the Bible's side.

# CHAPTER 18

# God Is Preparing Everyone for the Gospel

❦

I n my experience, I've often been amazed to see how God has gone to great length to prepare people to receive His message. One choice example took place in the early 1940s. A sheik named Rashed lived between Syria and Lebanon, where he ruled a Bedouin tribe of about twenty thousand people living in tents. He had the last word in everything that happened in the tribe. Missionaries and Bible salesmen would pass through, stopping to tell Bible stories to the illiterate sheik. He would marvel at what Isa (the Arabic word for "Jesus") could do.

In order to find enough food, Bedouin sheiks regularly raided other tribes, killing the men and taking their sheep, women, and children. After one such raid, Sheik Rashed returned home, ate a good meal, and then took a nap under a tree near his tent in the desert.

A venerable person in white with angry, piercing eyes appeared to him in a dream. Immediately Rashed realized that this was Jesus. "Lord Isa, what do You want with me?" pleaded Rashed in his dream. "Why are You angry with me?"

Jesus replied, "My dear Sheik Rashed, I have sent you so many people who have told you about My love for other people. But you still kill them. And you ask Me why I am angry with you?"

"Please tell me what I should do," said Rashed in his dream.

"Go to Jerusalem, and people there will tell you what to do," replied Jesus.

The next day Rashed rode his horse to Damascus, and then south to Jerusalem. But when he got there, he felt foolish because he did not know where to go or who would tell him about Isa.

Since it was hot, he went to a coffee shop to get something cold to drink. At an adjacent table he heard two men arguing. "Oh, He has not come yet. We are waiting for Him," said the first man.

"Oh, yes, He has come," said the second man, referring to the words of this prophet and that prophet that had been fulfilled. Rashed realized that the second man would be able to tell him about Isa. The two men stood up to pay. Rashed did, too, and followed them down the street. When the men separated, Rashed followed the second one and then knocked on his door soon after he entered.

This was the home of Ibraham, a Palestinian evangelist, who witnessed to Arabs and Jews even at the time when real trouble started between them over the Holy Land. Ibraham's wife opened the door to Rashed and slammed it shut at once. She thought that a fierce Bedouin had come to kill her husband because of his evangelistic activities.

From her description of the visitor, Ibraham realized that he was a Bedouin. Knowing their customs, Ibraham told his wife to welcome him in and to serve him food. If he ate, that meant he was a friend. If he rejected the food, that meant he was an enemy. Ibraham would wait in another room until she told him what happened. If the man refused to eat, Ibraham planned to jump out the window and run away.

Ibraham's wife opened the door, warmly welcoming the astonished sheik. He was even more perplexed when she brought him food. Hungry, he rolled up his sleeves, called on God's name, and began to eat.

"Ibraham! Ibraham! He's eating!" she shouted. Ibraham came

out and hugged the sheik as if he were an old friend, for he was used to the Bedouin ways. And then, God helped him lead the sheik to Christ that very day, and Rashed returned to his tribe a happy man.

In 1948 the Jews took part of Palestine to form the nation of Israel, so Ibraham was forced to go to Lebanon as a refugee. There I met him when he came to seek Bibles for his work. Soon Ibraham and I were visiting together often. We would go stay with the sheik's (Rashed's) clan for three to four days at a time. We would sleep on little mats in a tent that housed five people. We could feel scorpions walking under our mats. Our thin blankets had holes in them, but by using several blankets, the holes were covered up. All night long, chickens, roosters, cats, dogs, little goats, and lambs would run over us. We would wake up and see the morning stars through the holes in the tent.

If the sheik had only one goat when we arrived, he would kill it to feed us. And if Rashed felt a soft piece of meat in his mouth, one without gristle, he would take it out of his mouth and give it to us—his beloved guests. He hadn't heard about germs.

Women would resort to digging up wild potatoes and whatever they could find from the fields, because they didn't plant anything. In addition to what they found in the desert, they ate meat, yogurt, and cheese, which they themselves produced.

While the women prepared the food, Rashed sat in his tent to receive guests, going through the arduous steps to make them coffee. First he would make a fire with straw, dung, and thorns, which reeked and smoked up the tent until our eyes watered. Then, after roasting the coffee beans, he pounded them rhythmically in the hollowed center of a stone resting near him. In one of his three tall, brass pots sitting on stones, he would boil these smashed coffee beans for thirty minutes, adding cardamon and some of yesterday's coffee. After it settled, he would pour the top portion into a second brass pot for a half hour more of boiling and settling . . . and then into the third pot for the same. The end result was some two cups of coffee. And then he would repeat the process.

All the sheik's guests would sit in order of rank, and that is the order in which he served them. He poured three or four drops from the pot he held in his left hand into each of the three cups he owned, which he now held in his right hand, and he offered his first three guests one cup each. Everyone would drink to the last drop, savoring it fully, and then give his cup to the sheik for more.

This went on all day, with the small tent full of illiterate people. Ibraham and I would take turns reading the Scriptures for fifteen minutes at a time, all day. The people would ask simple questions, and often several of them received Christ.

People came and went all day, drinking coffee, listening to Bible stories. When a person had had enough coffee (it had to be an odd number of drinks—three or five or seven, etc.), he would tip the cup to face the sheik and move it in a slight circular fashion to indicate that he wanted no more. The sheik would then use the same cup to serve the next guest. At the end of the day, the sheik would rinse out the cups and dry them with the same part of his gown that he used to blow his nose or wipe something else!

Ibraham and I grew to be close friends. We arranged for one of Rashed's sons and one daughter to attend a Christian boarding school for Bedouin children.

Once Rashed was visiting me in my home. When he heard the radio, he asked, "Who's speaking inside?" I explained, but when I left the room, he picked up the tablecloth to see where the voice was really coming from. He remained faithful to the Lord to the end of his life.

I knew about a Christian mission in another land that wanted to build a hospital in a village on the Gulf. I went with the men in charge of the project to translate for them in asking the ruler of the area for property to build on. He said, ". . . on one condition: that you make it a mission hospital" (using the English word for mission and the Arabic word for hospital). They were astonished because that is exactly what they wanted.

After it was built, I went back to see the ruler repeatedly and once asked him why he had wanted a mission hospital. He did not even know what the word "mission" meant. "Even though I am the ruler, hospitals do not treat me with affection," he replied. "But at the mission hospital in Bahrain, I always felt at home and they treated me with so much love. This is what we need."

Samuel Zwemer, a missionary to Arabia in the nineteenth century, befriended the ruler's father, whom he had met when he was a patient at the mission hospital. He even gave him a Bible in the course of their friendship. As the father read the Bible, he called his children to tell them that Isaiah said the desert would blossom one day (Isaiah 35:4-7, 41:18-20, 43:18-21). "This is what is going to happen," he told them. But they secretly laughed at him.

A generation later, through the discovery of oil and the money the Gulf state was able to get from selling it, irrigation became possible. Then the desert blossomed. So the ruler said to me, "The Bible is true."

I said, "Will you permit me, Your Highness, to read you another passage from the prophet Isaiah?" He handed me his father's Bible and I read to him Isaiah 52:13–53:12. After I finished, he said with large, amazed eyes, "Isn't the prophet speaking here of our Lord Isa [Jesus]?" As I answered in the affirmative, he asked again, "Then why did he say that He was put to death, placed with evil men, and buried with the rich?" I explained to him how the Jews condemned Him to death, how the Roman soldiers nailed Him to the cross, and how Lord Isa asked God, before He died, to forgive all those who caused His death.

The ruler looked at me with a stern look in his eyes and some anguish in his voice and asked again, "But why did He die?" So I told him about Christ's death for our salvation and His resurrection and ascension to heaven, where He sits at God's right hand to intercede for us.

"Our Lord Isa did marvelous things, I know," he acknowledged. Seeing that the Holy Spirit was convincing him in a way I could never have convinced him myself, I told him, "He still does. He changed my life."

As I told him about my former life as a sinner and how Christ changed my life, he asked, "Will He change my life also as He did for you?" At my affirmative answer he said, "What do I have to do to obtain this new life?"

"Just ask Him," I said.

"I am not used to talking with Him," he said. "Please tell me what to say, and I will repeat after you." He put his hand in my two hands as I prayed. When we opened our eyes, tears were flowing down his cheeks.

And so, because of the loving care of the staff at the Bahrain Hospital, the friendship of Samuel Zwemer with his father, and my dozen visits to befriend this ruler, his heart was fertile soil for the good news. Every time I visited him after that, he would take me aside to read the Word and pray with him. He even helped me, on occasion, to fulfill my ministry.

So be encouraged. God is preparing people to receive the good news through you. You have only to trust Him and open your ears to His voice as He leads you. Go forward with Him, without any wavering.

# AUTHOR

As a child in Lebanon, FOUAD ELIAS ACCAD wondered why the Bible was chained to the pulpit of the Greek Orthodox church he attended. He thought perhaps it was a book of sorcery. In his teens he got his hands on a copy of the Bible, which was forbidden to all but the priests in his church. In this Bible he secretly read the truth about Jesus Christ.

It seemed to him that no one else knew of the importance of the Bible. But one day while in his late teens, Fouad discovered that there were followers of Jesus who openly carried Bibles around with them, searching the pages to discover God's truth. This was the same book that Fouad had been secretly reading. But suddenly he had many friends who prayed to God and found in the Bible answers to their deepest questions. Fouad found that in Jesus Christ there was life-changing Truth. As a result, he felt that his calling in life was to set the Word of God free.

It became clear to Fouad that a primary need in his country was to "unchain" the Bible. He and his Swiss wife, Suzanne, spent their lives reaching out to Muslims to give them the Bible's truths. Fouad became an ordained pastor, and was a scholar who knew ancient Hebrew, Greek, Syriac, Aramaic, and Armenian. In his later years, he was a respected *hakeem*, or "wise one," and so unique doors were opened to him. He befriended many important people, including sheiks and government officials in the Middle East. Fouad used passages from the Qur'an to show Muslims the truth of the Bible. He poured out his life in that quest until his death in 1994.

# LEARN THE ART OF SHARING CHRIST WITH OTHERS.

### Your Home a Lighthouse

Church can be overwhelming for nonChristians.
This book demonstrates how to lead an evangelistic Bible study in your own home,
giving unbelievers a glimpse of Christ in a comfortable setting.

*Your Home a Lighthouse*
(Bob & Betty Jacks with Ron Wormser, Sr.) $11

### The Power of Story

Everyone has a story to tell. Learn how telling the story of God's work
and influence in your life can help lead others to salvation in Christ.

*The Power of Story*
(Leighton Ford) $12

### Living Proof

Evangelism isn't as scary as it sounds. If you want to reach out to others,
this book will help you learn how to be living proof of the gospel
for nonChristian friends, neighbors, and coworkers.

*Living Proof*
(Jim Petersen) $12

### Lifestyle Discipleship

You've just led someone to Christ, now what? Learn how discipleship
can produce truly mature followers of Christ who, in turn, lead others to God.

*Lifestyle Discipleship*
(Jim Petersen) $12

Get your copies today at your local bookstore,
through our website, or by calling (800) 366-7788.
(Ask for offer **#2347** or a FREE catalog of NavPress products.)